In This Issue

PIVOT MAGAZINE

Founder
Jason Miller

President
Juddene Villarin

Web Master
Joel Phillips

Designs
ReliableStaffSolutions.com

Copyright © 2025 PIVOT

ISBN: 978-1-957217-90-1

Contact
Jason Miller
Founder
1151 Eagle Drive #345
Loveland, CO 80537
jason@strategicadvisorboard.com

Shelby Jo Long
Editor-in-Chief
shelby@strategicadvisorboard.com
877-944-0944

From the Editor

Building Stronger Foundations in an Era of Accountability

We're stepping into a business climate that demands more than ambition. It demands accountability.

This month's issue of Pivot unpacks a critical reality: the rules are changing, and the spotlight on leadership is brighter than ever. From navigating the legal pressures amplified during the Trump administration to rethinking governance, ethics, and corporate culture, this edition challenges leaders to lead smarter, sharper, and with deeper integrity.

Inside these pages, you'll find conversations that don't just highlight risk—they spotlight opportunity. Opportunity to refine your operations, strengthen your leadership frameworks, and build organizations that don't just survive scrutiny, but rise because of it.

Progress isn't just about chasing growth. It's about fortifying the foundation underneath it. And those who build wisely in this season will be the ones who lead the future.

Stay sharp. Stay principled. Stay ahead.

Shelby Jo Long
Editor-in-Chief

From the Desk
Of The President

Leading with Clarity When the Stakes Are Higher

This issue could not be more timely.

Across industries, the pressure on leadership is growing. Legal accountability, ethical governance, and organizational resilience are no longer optional. They are the new standard. The best leaders are not scrambling to react. They are anticipating, adapting, and leading with clarity through uncertainty.

At Pivot, we believe leadership is not just about managing success. It is about building strength that lasts under scrutiny.

The lessons throughout this issue are clear. Governance is strategy. Integrity is leverage. Culture is a competitive advantage.

As you move forward this quarter, ask yourself:

- Where are the cracks in your foundation that demand attention
- How can compliance become a strength, not just an obligation
- What principles will define your leadership when pressure builds

This is not the time to retreat. It is the time to refine.

Let us lead with conviction and build legacies that endure beyond the headlines.

JUDDENE VILLARIN

J.V.

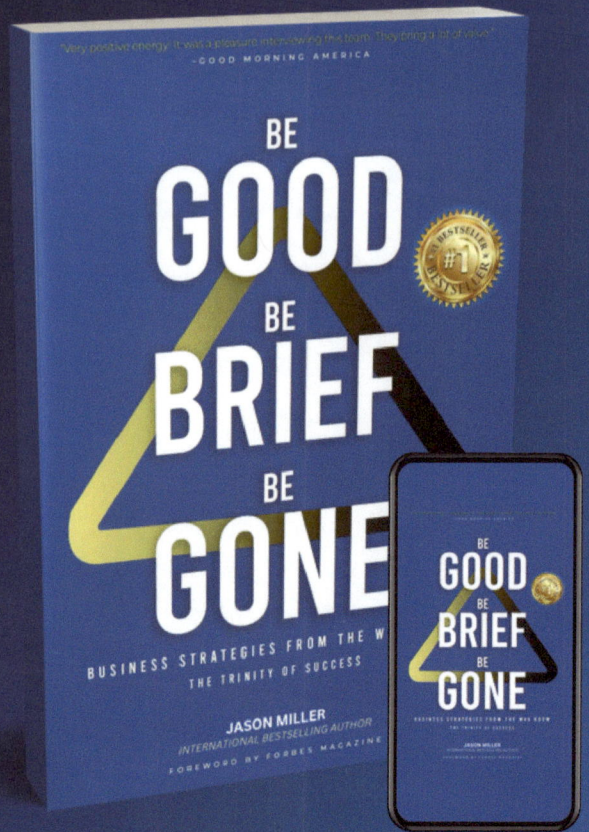
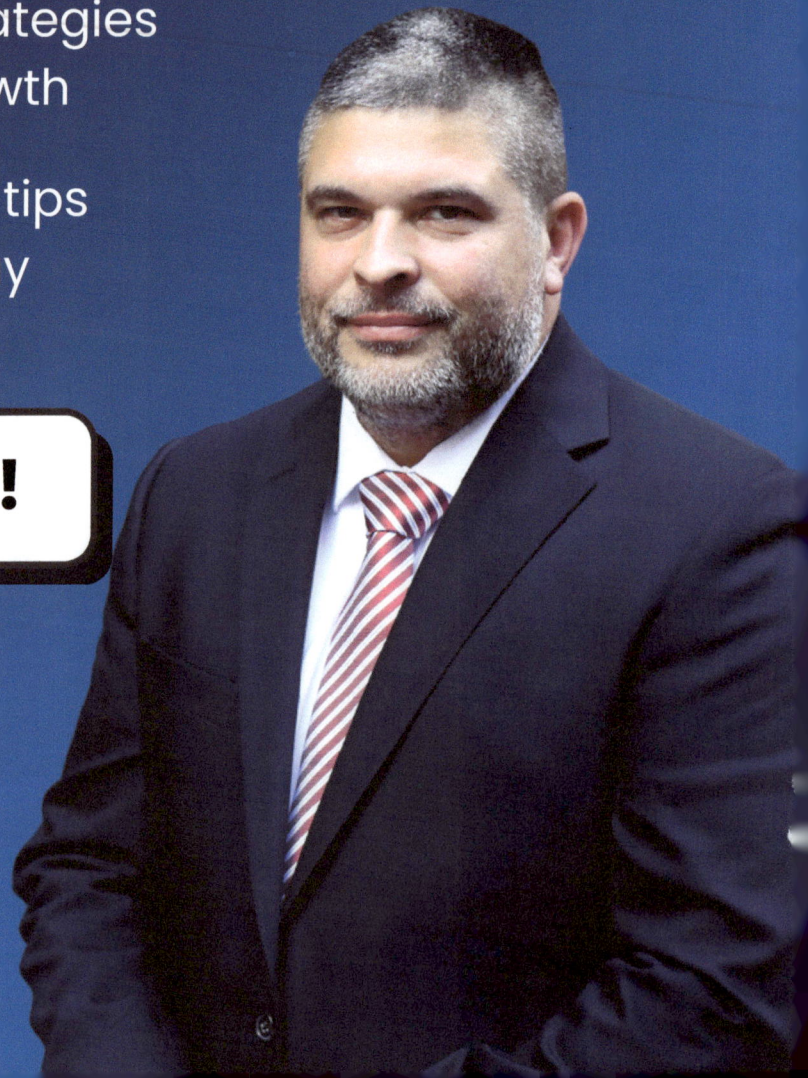

Investing in Sports Memorabilia as an Alternative Investment

"In recent years, investing in sports memorabilia has evolved from a niche hobby to a serious alternative investment class"

according to Bruce Fromong, a prominent sports agent to many legends of the past. Bruce further goes on to explain "As both a collector and investor myself, I like to point out to people that while it may be cost prohibitively to invest in rookie autographed cards of many vintage players they can still affordably do so in a current card of that same player that will present the potential for great financial growth that can offer the pleasure of owning their favorite player.

Example, while a 1965 Joe Namath rookie autographed perfect graded 10/10 card could run well over a quarter million dollars, a current autographed graded card of his could run as low as $2500". What was once the domain of passionate fans and collectors has now attracted the attention of wealthy investors looking for new opportunities beyond traditional asset classes like stocks, bonds, or real estate. Sports memorabilia, from jerseys and autographed baseballs to vintage tickets and game-worn items, has shown the potential for significant returns. As the global market for these collectibles grows, it's worth exploring the ins and outs of investing in sports memorabilia and its potential as an alternative investment strategy. Jason Miller and Bruce Fromong have partnered and created the Mint Card Vault to do just this for clients.

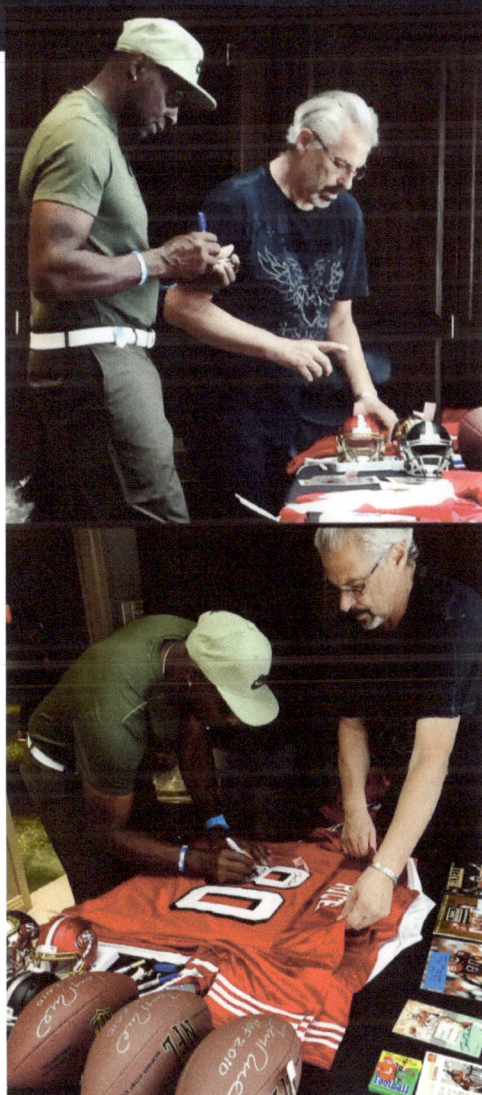

What is Sports Memorabilia?

Sports memorabilia encompasses a wide range of items associated with sports, athletes, and memorable events in the world of sports. These items include, but are not limited to, autographed jerseys, game-worn equipment, signed baseballs, vintage trading cards, ticket stubs, programs, and photographs. They hold value primarily due to their association with a specific player, team, or significant moment in sporting history. "The value of a piece of memorabilia can be influenced by several factors, including the rarity of the item, the stature of the athlete, and the historical significance of the event tied to it", Bruce comments.

The Rise of Sports Memorabilia as an Investment

Historically, sports memorabilia was seen as a collectible market, often associated with fans wanting to own a piece of sports history. However, the past few decades have witnessed a transformation. The shift from mere fanfare to investment has been driven by several key factors:

1. **Appreciation of Value:** In the past, collectors have seen significant returns on their investments. For example, a signed baseball from Babe Ruth sold for $200,000 in 1999. By 2019, that same baseball could be worth over $1 million. Similarly, rare trading cards, such as a 1952 Mickey Mantle card, have seen prices skyrocket, moving from modest sums to auction prices in the millions.

2. **Rarity and Demand:** The principle of supply and demand plays a significant role in determining the value of memorabilia. Items tied to legendary athletes like Michael Jordan, Muhammad Ali, and Jackie Robinson, for example, tend to hold exceptional value due to their rarity and cultural significance. As more collectors enter the market, the demand for these items grows, driving prices even higher.

3. **Emotional and Nostalgic Appeal:** For many investors, the appeal of sports memorabilia is not only financial but also emotional. Owning a piece of history that brings nostalgia and connects them to their favorite athletes or teams can be priceless. This emotional value can sometimes push prices higher than traditional investment models might predict.

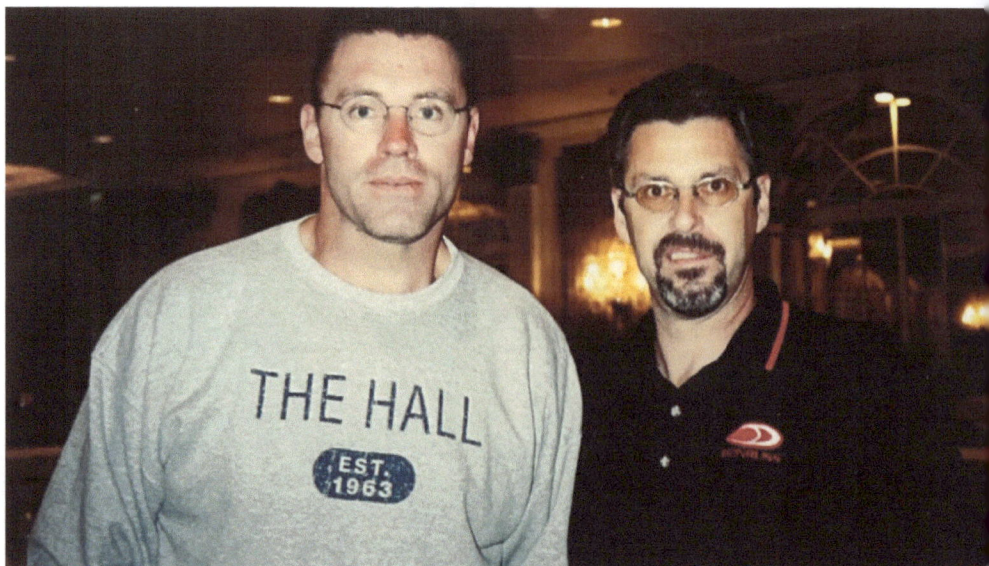

4. Celebrity and Social Media Influence: Athletes today are more prominent than ever, thanks in large part to social media. High-profile athletes like LeBron James, Tom Brady, and Serena Williams are icons, and their memorabilia carries a level of prestige that has boosted its demand. Social media platforms allow these athletes to connect directly with fans and collectors, further increasing the visibility and desirability of their memorabilia.

5. Auction Houses and Online Platforms: The advent of online auction platforms and niche marketplaces such as eBay, Heritage Auctions, and even fractional ownership sites like Rally Road has made it easier than ever for investors to buy and sell sports memorabilia. These platforms have broadened the market, enabling investors to access rare items that might have previously been out of reach.

The Financial Potential of Sports Memorabilia

"Sports memorabilia can serve as a unique investment, often providing returns that outperform traditional asset classes", in Jason's opinion. The market for collectibles has been particularly strong in the past decade, with high-value items fetching millions of dollars at auction. The financial potential of sports memorabilia as an investment can be broken down into several factors:

1. Long-Term Growth: Collectibles, including sports memorabilia, have shown long-term growth potential. While markets for more traditional assets such as stocks or bonds can fluctuate, sports memorabilia tends to experience gradual appreciation over time, particularly for items tied to legends of the sport. Items that were once considered "junk" or "mass-produced," like trading cards from the 1980s and 1990s, are now being re-evaluated for their historical significance and rarity.

2. Diversification: Like other alternative investments, sports memorabilia offers diversification away from traditional markets. As with any investment, diversification is essential for reducing risk, and sports memorabilia can serve as a hedge against stock market volatility or inflation. The performance of this asset class often behaves independently of the broader financial markets, making it an attractive option for investors seeking stability in uncertain economic times.

3. Access to High-Value Items: While some sports memorabilia can be prohibitively expensive (such as iconic jerseys worn by legendary athletes or championship rings), the rise of fractional ownership platforms allows investors to buy into high-value assets without having to purchase the entire item. This has opened up the market to a broader range of investors, further increasing liquidity and the potential for profit.

Risks and Challenges of Investing in Sports Memorabilia

While the upside potential of sports memorabilia is appealing, it's important for investors to understand the risks and challenges that come with this alternative asset class. Here are some of the key considerations:

1. Market Volatility: The sports memorabilia market is not immune to economic cycles. Economic downturns, shifts in consumer preferences, and changes in the sports landscape can all affect the market's stability. For instance, a decline in an athlete's reputation or a significant scandal could decrease the value of their memorabilia.

2. Authenticity and Condition: The value of sports memorabilia is often tied to its condition and authenticity. Investors must be vigilant in verifying the provenance of their items to avoid purchasing counterfeit or altered memorabilia. Certificates of authenticity (COAs) and expert appraisals are crucial in establishing an item's legitimacy. In addition, the preservation of items is critical to maintaining their value. Items that are not properly stored or are exposed to environmental factors like humidity, light, or dust can deteriorate over time.

3. Illiquidity: Unlike stocks or bonds, sports memorabilia can be illiquid, meaning it may take time to sell the items at a desirable price. There is no guarantee that an item will sell quickly or for the expected price. Investors must be prepared for the fact that they may need to wait years to realize the full financial potential of their investments.

4. Lack of Regulation: The sports memorabilia market is less regulated compared to traditional financial markets, which can create uncertainty. The absence of clear pricing standards or regulations can make it difficult to assess the fair market value of certain items, and the market can sometimes be driven by speculation rather than intrinsic value.

Investing in sports memorabilia offers a unique and potentially lucrative opportunity for alternative asset diversification. The combination of nostalgia, rarity, and historical significance can create an attractive investment vehicle with the potential for impressive returns.

However, as with any investment, there are risks involved, including market volatility, authenticity issues, and the illiquidity of certain items. For those willing to research, understand, and navigate these challenges, sports memorabilia can be a compelling and rewarding addition to an investment portfolio.

Whether you are a passionate collector or an investor looking to diversify your assets, sports memorabilia represent a vibrant and growing market with the potential to deliver both financial and personal satisfaction. As the market continues to expand, now may be a prime time to get involved and secure a piece of sports history for both investment and enjoyment.

RSS›
Reliable Staff Solutions

STAFF SPOTLIGHT

Behind the Vision: Rold Reyes
From Junior Publicist to Full-Stack Marketer

"Working at RSS has taught me that, when you keep an open mind to continuous learning and an open heart to unleashing your creative potential, great things happen."

When did you join the RSS team, and what brought you here?

June 2022

What's your favorite part of working at RSS?

Teamwork, growth, challenge.

How has your role evolved since you started?

From pitching to redesigning brands!

Describe your typical workday or work-from-home setup

Dependable, focused, proactive

If you could describe RSS in three words, what would they be?

Reliable, Steadfast, Family

STAFF STATS

☕ Go to drink: Warm tea (black green, or chamomile)

🎧 Work Anthem: Stronger by Kanye West

🍪 Favorite Snack: Pastries

💡 Fun Fact: Speaks at universities on journalism. design, & marketing

"

Reliable isn't just a word. It's how we show up for our team and for our clients.

Be a Genius Entrepreneur

Live a life of freedom, optimum performance, and passion.

Genius Entrepreneur group

- ✔ Weekly zoom meetings
- ✔ Community of Support
- ✔ Marketing opportunities

Genius Entrepreneur Program

- ✔ Brand Strategy
- ✔ Signature Program
- ✔ Rogram curriculum

Genius Speaker Series

- ✔ Keynote Speaker training
- ✔ Tedx Training
- ✔ Sell from stage

SHELBY JO LONG
BUSINESS COACHING

Shelbyjolong.com | Business Dynamics

How to Align Digital Transformation with Business Goals and Strategy

In today's competitive landscape, digital transformation is more than just a buzzword—it's a critical element for staying relevant, responsive, and sustainable. With industries evolving rapidly due to technological innovation, businesses must make intentional moves to adopt digital tools that enhance operations, elevate customer experience, and drive growth.

However, success doesn't come from adopting the latest tech alone. The real key lies in aligning digital transformation with your business goals and overall strategy. Without this alignment, even the most sophisticated platforms, systems, or tools may fail to deliver meaningful outcomes or generate long-term impact.

Prioritizing Digital Transformation as a Strategic Imperative

Digital transformation should be embedded within an

This integration is what allows a company to adapt and grow in step with evolving market demands. Unfortunately, many businesses still approach digitalization reactively, launching tools without a strong connection to strategy.

Senior leaders often acknowledge digital transformation as a priority, but too often, execution falls flat due to a lack of strategic clarity. Studies show that while over 80% of companies invest in digital tools, only a fraction achieve measurable transformation across business functions. This misalignment creates a disconnect between investment and impact.

To bridge this gap, leadership must start by asking: What are our business goals? What role should digital innovation play in achieving them?

Let's say a company's goal is to grow its client base by 30% within 12 months. To support this, it might invest in marketing automation, lead scoring AI, or CRM integration to streamline outreach and improve follow-up efficiency. For a commercial low voltage contractor, this could mean adopting digital project tracking, smart inventory systems, or augmented reality for on-site installations. Each digital move should have a direct, measurable link to a strategic objective.

Digital transformation in specialized industries also demands customized communication across leadership tiers. For example:

- Executives need to understand the ROI and strategic alignment.

- Middle managers want to see how it enhances workflow and KPIs.

- Frontline staff must be shown how it makes their job easier or safer.

Without clear communication and stakeholder buy-in across these levels, digital efforts may face resistance or stagnation.

Setting Clear Objectives to Drive Success

Digital transformation often stumbles not because of poor tools, but because of vague direction. Without clearly defined objectives, digital projects tend to become disconnected experiments that fail to scale or deliver return.

The foundation of success lies in goal-setting that is:

- **Specific:** Clearly define the purpose. Is it about reducing response time? Increasing upsell revenue? Streamlining operations?

- **Measurable:** Set KPIs and performance benchmarks.

- **Achievable:** Ensure internal capabilities and resources can support the initiative.

- **Relevant:** Objectives must directly align with overarching business goals.

- **Time-bound:** Attach timelines for assessment and review.

For example, an e-commerce business may set an objective to increase cart conversion rates by 10% over the next quarter.

A digital strategy aligned with this goal may include A/B testing, chatbot support during checkout, and dynamic pricing algorithms.

Another layer to consider is agility. Digital transformation isn't static—it evolves. Businesses should revisit goals periodically, allowing room to pivot when market dynamics shift.

Organizations that revisit their digital objectives quarterly or bi-annually tend to see more measurable growth, as they remain proactive instead of reactive. This regular recalibration helps keep all efforts aligned and relevant.

Measuring ROI and Ensuring Continuous Improvement

One of the biggest challenges organizations face during digital transformation is accurately measuring return on investment (ROI). Unlike traditional projects where success might be evident in short-term gains or immediate cost savings, digital transformation often delivers value in more abstract or long-term ways. ROI in this context isn't always immediate or linear —it unfolds gradually as new technologies are adopted and begin to influence broader operational dynamics. Understanding this delayed payoff is crucial for setting realistic expectations and maintaining leadership buy-in throughout the process.

A perfect example of this is customer relationship management (CRM) system integration. Initially, the rollout of a new CRM platform can disrupt routines and workflows, slowing teams down as they undergo training and adapt to a different way of working.

These early inefficiencies might be misinterpreted as signs of failure. However, over time, the system can start delivering significant returns—such as reducing customer churn, improving retention rates, and streamlining the sales cycle. The real ROI emerges not from the technology itself, but from the improved decision-making, personalized customer interactions, and strategic insights it enables.

To ensure these benefits are realized, it's important to implement continuous improvement frameworks alongside digital transformation initiatives. This involves setting clear KPIs from the start—not only focusing on financial outcomes but also operational and experiential metrics. For example, tracking user adoption rates, employee engagement, customer satisfaction, and process efficiency can all provide a more holistic view of progress. These metrics offer a way to capture early wins, identify areas of resistance, and iterate in real time to keep momentum going.

Additionally, embracing a culture of agility and feedback is essential. As teams interact with new tools, their feedback can help refine implementation strategies and maximize functionality. Regular review cycles, where both successes and setbacks are discussed, create an environment of learning and growth. In this way, the transformation becomes not just a one-time project, but an ongoing evolution that adapts to market demands and internal insights. Empowering employees to take part in shaping how new tools are used reinforces engagement and deepens the long-term impact.

Ultimately, measuring ROI in digital transformation goes beyond spreadsheets and bottom lines—it requires a strategic lens that captures both tangible and intangible gains. While the upfront investment in time, training, and technology may seem steep, the long-term benefits often far outweigh the initial cost. By focusing on continuous improvement, maintaining a flexible approach, and being patient with the learning curve, organizations can unlock sustained value and build a more resilient, future-ready operation.

Consider this ROI tracking example for a healthcare company digitizing patient intake:

- Short term: 20% reduction in wait times within 60 days.

- Medium term: 15% drop in appointment no-shows.

- Long term: 30% increase in patient satisfaction scores over 12 months.

Importantly, digital transformation should be seen as a journey, not a fixed project with a defined start and end point. It's not simply a matter of installing new software or automating a few processes—true transformation involves a fundamental shift in how a business thinks, operates, and delivers value. This journey requires a long-term vision, but also the flexibility to adapt along the way. As markets evolve and new technologies emerge, so too must the strategies and systems that organizations rely on. Leaders must accept that transformation is never really "done," but rather an ongoing commitment to innovation, learning, and improvement.

To truly transform, businesses must ditch static annual reports for real-time feedback tools—dashboards, analytics, and check-ins—that fuel continuous improvement and make adaptability a built-in strength.

Traditional vs. Digitally Aligned Strategies

Element	Traditional Strategy	Digitally Aligned Strategy
Customer Interaction	Call centers, physical forms	AI chatbots, omnichannel platforms
Sales & Marketing	Print ads, cold calling	Automated campaigns, predictive analytics
Operations	Manual tracking, siloed teams	Integrated ERP systems, real-time dashboards
Decision Making	Gut feel, experience-led	Data-driven, scenario modeling
Product Development	Long cycles, waterfall approach	Agile, iterative innovation
Employee Training	In-person sessions, static manuals	eLearning, virtual simulations
Scaling	High cost, regional limits	Cloud-based systems, global scalability

This comparison illustrates how aligning digital tools with strategic goals leads to improved flexibility, efficiency, and growth potential.

To manage expectations and effectively track ROI:

- **Set performance benchmarks early:** These should align with goals such as customer satisfaction, cycle time reduction, or revenue per customer.

- **Use both qualitative and quantitative data:** Monitor operational KPIs, but also collect staff feedback and customer testimonials.

- **Identify short-term wins and long-term growth:** For example, while cost savings might be long-term, productivity boosts could be observed within the first 90 days.

Best Practices for Strategic Digital Transformation

To ensure a smooth and strategic approach:

- **Audit before action:** Map current processes and identify pain points.

- **Build a digital roadmap:** This should include short-term wins and long-term evolution.

- **Create a change champion team:** Select cross-functional leaders who will advocate, train, and drive adoption.

- **Invest in culture:** Foster a mindset of experimentation, feedback, and adaptation.

Overcoming Common Challenges in Digital Transformation Alignment

Even with the best-laid plans, obstacles will arise. Here are key challenges and how to navigate them:

1. Resistance to Change
Change can trigger fear—fear of job loss, skill irrelevance, or increased workload. To overcome this, involve employees early. Explain how digital tools make their roles more efficient, not obsolete. Invest in training and highlight early wins.

2. Lack of Scalability
Many companies launch pilot programs but fail to scale due o lack of planning. Avoid this by building scalable infrastructure from the start. Cloud platforms, modular systems, and flexible APIs allow you to adapt and grow.

3. Siloed Efforts
Digital transformation cannot live in IT alone. It must cross departments, tying into sales, marketing, HR, and customer support. Create cross-functional transformation teams to ensure unified planning and execution.

4. Poor Vendor Management
Too often, businesses get tied into vendor systems without considering long-term flexibility. Be intentional about vendor relationships—prioritize integrations, portability, and support.

5. Misaligned KPIs
Avoid the trap of vanity metrics (e.g., downloads, clicks) that don't relate to core goals. Focus on actionable indicators tied to strategic outcomes: revenue, retention, margin, and satisfaction.

- **Secure leadership alignment:** Without buy-in from the top, transformation stalls. Leaders must sponsor and model change.

Case Study: Digital Alignment in Action

Company:
A regional logistics firm

Challenge:
Missed delivery deadlines, rising customer complaints

Goal:
Improve delivery accuracy and customer satisfaction by 25%

Digital Moves:

- Adopted GPS fleet tracking

- Integrated CRM for real-time updates

- Launched customer portal for shipment visibility

Results:

- 35% improvement in on-time deliveries

- 20% rise in client retention

- 18% reduction in customer service inquiries

FAQs

How can businesses ensure that their digital transformation initiatives are aligned with their strategic goals?

By embedding measurable, outcome-focused objectives that directly relate to business growth or efficiency. Regular checkpoints and performance reviews help maintain alignment over time.

What are common challenges in aligning digital transformation with business goals?

Resistance to change, lack of cross-functional collaboration, and poor communication. These can be tackled through internal champions, regular training, and a clear roadmap.

How do you measure digital transformation ROI?

Focus on strategic KPIs such as cost per acquisition, ustomer lifetime value, employee productivity, and satisfaction metrics. Long-term gains should be tracked alongside immediate wins.

What role does leadership play in digital transformation?

Leadership drives vision and culture. Leaders must endorse and model the change to ensure organization-wide commitment and alignment.

Can small businesses also implement aligned digital transformation?

Yes—often more easily than large enterprises. With fewer layers and more flexibility, small businesses can experiment quickly and pivot as needed. The key is to align every tech investment with a growth or efficiency goal.

Conclusion

Aligning digital transformation with business goals is not a luxury—it's a necessity for growth and relevance. It ensures that investments in technology deliver strategic value, not just operational novelty.

To succeed, businesses must:

- Prioritize digital initiatives within strategic planning

- Set and review clear objectives

- Measure outcomes beyond surface-level ROI

- Scale intentionally while addressing cultural and process-related barriers

Digital transformation is not about tools. It's about transforming the business model itself—how you serve, how you operate, how you compete. When digital initiatives are grounded in strategy, they become a powerful engine for innovation, efficiency, and long-term value.

The Role of Storytelling in Effective Brand Strategy

In today's saturated markets, connecting with customers isn't optional—it's the foundation for sustainable brand success. Customers are constantly bombarded with ads, promotions, and offers. So, what separates a memorable brand from a forgettable one? It's not just about product features, pricing, or distribution —it's about how the brand makes people feel. And the most powerful way to spark emotion and connection is through storytelling.

Great brands don't just sell; they share narratives that resonate. Whether it's the origin of the brand, the people behind it, or the transformation customers experience when using the product—storytelling builds emotional bridges between brands and people. It invites customers into a bigger vision, where the product becomes part of their identity or aspiration.

Let's explore the key roles storytelling plays in brand strategy, along with practical ways to integrate it into your marketing efforts.

1. Creating Emotional Connections That Stick

Emotion drives behavior more than logic ever could. In fact, according to a Harvard study, 95% of purchasing decisions are subconscious—driven largely by emotion, not rational analysis.

A compelling story taps into values, memories, hopes, or fears that customers already hold. When your brand narrative your audience relates to— whether it's perseverance, creativity, belonging, or empowerment—it builds an emotional tie that advertising alone can't achieve.

Example: Dove's "Real Beauty" campaign didn't focus on soap or body wash. It told stories about real women challenging beauty standards, sparking a movement that made people care deeply about the brand's purpose. That

emotional hook has helped Dove maintain brand relevance for decades.

Practical Tip: Use storytelling to highlight customer success stories, challenges overcome, or founder journeys. Make it relatable and personal. Emotionally connected customers are more loyal and willing to advocate for your brand.

2. Humanizing the Brand

People buy from people—not logos. That's why showing the human side of your brand is vital. Storytelling helps you peel back the corporate façade and show the real people, struggles, and values behind the business.

When a brand feels authentic, customers feel they're engaging with a community, not just a product. It's about demonstrating that your brand has a soul, a purpose, and real people who care.

Example: Patagonia is a masterclass in this approach. Their stories of environmental activism, employee adventures, and ethical sourcing have positioned them as more than just an apparel brand. Their transparency makes customers feel proud to support them.

Practical Tip: Share behind-the-scenes content, founder stories, team highlights, or day-in-the-life snippets. Show the messy, real, imperfect journey. Vulnerability builds trust.

3. Differentiating Your Brand in a Crowded Market

In markets flooded with similar products, differentiation is no longer about specs—it's about story.

The truth is, very few products are truly unique. But a compelling brand narrative can elevate even the most commoditized item into something distinctive and desirable.

Example: Think about TOMS Shoes. The product itself—basic canvas footwear—wasn't revolutionary. But the "One for One" story gave it meaning. For every pair sold, a child in need received one. That story created instant emotional investment and market differentiation.

Practical Tip: Craft a brand origin story that highlights a unique mission, moment of inspiration, or personal struggle. Even small brands can stand out with the right narrative.

4. Strengthening Brand Identity and Values

Stories don't just entertain—they teach. They're an effective way to reinforce your brand's mission, values, and vision without sounding preachy or promotional.

By illustrating what your brand stands for through storytelling, you help customers understand

who you are, what you care about, and why they should care too.

Example: Ben & Jerry's shares stories around social justice, climate change, and economic equity. Their storytelling aligns with their identity as an activist brand, and their customer base reflects that shared value system.

Practical Tip: Instead of listing values on a website, illustrate them through stories—customer journeys, community initiatives, employee experiences. Let your actions do the storytelling.

5. Driving Shareability and Organic Reach

People don't share ads—they share stories. A compelling narrative has a natural viral factor because it invites conversation, empathy, and reflection.

Story-driven content is far more likely to be shared on social media, discussed in forums, or featured in media outlets. This amplifies reach organically and helps brands build communities rather than just traffic.

Example: Airbnb's "Belong Anywhere" campaign featured hosts and guests sharing powerful stories of connection and cultural exchange. These weren't commercials—they were mini documentaries, sparking engagement and shares across platforms.

Practical Tip: Tell stories in formats your audience loves—short videos, carousels, blog posts, podcasts. Focus on moments that evoke curiosity, joy, or empathy.

6. Inspiring Action and Purchase Decisions

Good stories don't just create awareness—they drive action. When customers see themselves as part of your brand's journey, they're more likely to take the next step: purchase, donate, share, or sign up.

This is especially impactful for mission-driven brands or those engaged in social impact. Stories of real change help customers feel like participants in a greater purpose.

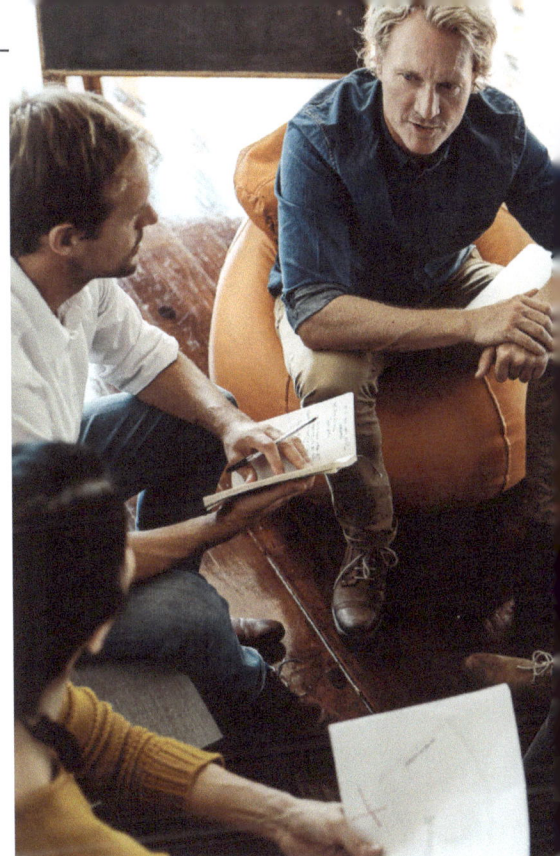

Example: Warby Parker made buying glasses feel like activism. Their stories around global eye care access inspired customers to take action beyond the transaction.

Practical Tip: Build your call-to-action into the story arc. Don't just pitch—invite. Use phrases like "join us," "be part of," or "help us make an impact."

7. Building Long-Term Loyalty Through Story Arcs

One great story may spark interest—but a consistent stream of stories creates deep loyalty. Think of storytelling as building a relationship, not a one-time campaign.

When your audience can follow your journey—your growth, challenges, wins—they feel like insiders. This sense of belonging increases customer lifetime value, repeat purchases, and advocacy.

Example: Glossier has built a cult following through stories of real customers, behind-the-scenes product development, and founder Emily Weiss's own entrepreneurial journey.

Practical Tip: Develop a storytelling calendar. Instead of separate, siloed stories, create ongoing arcs—brand chapters, seasonal stories, or character spotlights.

8. Elevating Product Perception

A strong narrative can dramatically increase perceived value. When people know the story behind a product—where it comes from, who made it, what inspired it—they're more likely to view it as premium or purposeful.

Example: Luxury brands like Rolex and Hermes lean heavily on heritage storytelling. The craftsmanship, legacy, and artistry behind their products justify premium pricing and status.

Practical Tip: For each product, share the "why" behind its creation. Use packaging, product pages, and video content to deepen the narrative and enhance perceived value.

9. Empowering Customers to Tell Their Own Stories

The most powerful brand stories are the ones customers tell for you. When you invite them to be part of your narrative, they become co-creators—and ambassadors.

User-generated content, reviews, testimonials, and unboxing experiences all contribute to your brand's living story. Encourage this participation and highlight their stories.

Example: GoPro built its brand on user-generated storytelling. Customers' adventurous videos became the brand's most powerful marketing tool.

Practical Tip: Feature customer stories across your platforms. Run storytelling challenges or invite submissions around how they use your product. Make your customers the hero.

10. Boosting Internal Alignment and Culture

Storytelling isn't just external—it also strengthens your internal brand. Sharing stories within your team helps align employees with the mission and creates a unified culture.

When your team understands and believes in the brand story, they become better ambassadors, collaborators, and decision-makers.

Example: Zappos regularly shares customer service stories internally to reinforce its value of delivering happiness. This fuels motivation and culture alignment.

Practical Tip: Use storytelling in onboarding, internal newsletters, or meetings. Share stories of customer wins, employee contributions, or moments that reflect your values.

Integrating Storytelling into Your Brand Strategy

Storytelling isn't just a buzzword—it's a powerful way to build emotional connections, differentiate your brand, and inspire loyalty. Ready to weave compelling narratives into your brand strategy? Here's a more detailed roadmap to get started:

Step 1: Define Your Core Narrative

Start with the heart of your brand. What's your origin story? What problem were you trying to solve? Who are the people behind the brand, and what inspired them? This foundational story should reflect your mission, vision, and values—the essence that all future content can grow from. A strong core narrative acts as your storytelling North Star, guiding tone, messaging, and direction across all platforms.

Step 2: Know Your Audience Inside and Out

Great storytelling speaks directly to the listener's heart. Go beyond demographics—dig into psychographics. What motivates your audience? What are their fears, dreams, daily struggles, and long-term aspirations? Craft stories that mirror their experiences, reflect their values, and offer hope or solutions. Empathy is your storytelling superpower.

Example: GoPro built its brand on user-generated storytelling. Customers' adventurous videos became the brand's most powerful marketing tool.

Practical Tip: Feature customer stories across your platforms. Run storytelling challenges or invite submissions around how they use your product. Make your customers the hero.

Step 3: Identify Your Story Pillars

Think of these as the recurring themes or values your brand consistently explores. These might include innovation, resilience, sustainability, craftsmanship, community, empowerment, or adventure. Establishing story pillars gives your content direction and cohesion, helping audiences recognize what your brand stands for—no matter the format or platform.

Step 4: Choose the Right Medium for the Message

Not every story belongs on every channel. A behind-the-scenes manufacturing journey might shine in a mini-documentary, while a customer success story might work better as an Instagram carousel or blog post. Match the medium to the message and the audience's habits. Consider a mix of formats—videos, podcasts, newsletters, case studies, social reels—to bring your stories to life in diverse, digestible ways.

Step 5: Keep It Authentic and Human

Audiences can spot a fake from a mile away. Drop the corporate jargon and let real voices shine through. Share wins, but also talk about missteps, lessons learned, and the messy middle of growth. Vulnerability builds trust. The more human your stories feel, the more likely people are to connect, remember, and advocate for your brand.

Conclusion

In a marketplace where attention is scarce and trust is fragile, storytelling is one of the most powerful tools a brand can use. It transforms products into experiences, customers into communities, and businesses into movements.

Whether you're a startup trying to find your voice or an established brand seeking deeper loyalty, storytelling isn't optional—it's strategic. It's what turns marketing into meaning.

By crafting authentic, engaging, and value-driven narratives, you don't just attract customers—you build relationships that last.

Maximizing Client Engagement Through Effective Email Practices

Despite the explosion of social media platforms and a growing ecosystem of messaging apps, email remains a cornerstone of digital communication—and one of the most reliable and cost-effective marketing tools available to businesses today. While newer channels may come and go, email consistently delivers high ROI, thanks to its unique ability to reach audiences directly, scale effortlessly, and provide clear, measurable performance metrics.

What sets email apart isn't just its longevity—it's its versatility. Whether you're nurturing leads, building long-term trust, or converting prospects into loyal, paying customers, email has the power to move the needle at every stage of the customer journey. It can feel personal, even when sent en masse. It can inform, persuade, and delight—all in a single message.

However, in today's hyper-connected world, simply hitting "send" isn't enough. Inboxes are battlegrounds, crowded with promotional clutter, unread newsletters, and auto-generated alerts. The challenge? Standing out. And that means delivering content that is not just relevant and timely, but engaging—content that resonates with your audience and makes them want to click, read, and act.

This is where strategy meets execution. Crafting a compelling email campaign requires more than catchy subject lines and attractive visuals. t demands a thoughtful approach, rooted in best practices that help ensure your messages actually reach their destination—and don't end up in the spam abyss.

In this comprehensive guide, we'll walk you through a series of actionable steps you can take to elevate your email engagement strategy. From segmentation and personalization to crafting irresistible CTAs, we'll cover the fundamentals that drive performance. But we'll also shine a spotlight on a critical, often underestimated factor in email success: **email verification**.

Yes, it might not sound glamorous —but verifying your email list can be the difference between a campaign that performs and one that falls flat. We'll explain why it matters, how it works, and how you can use verification tools to maintain a clean list, improve deliverability, and protect your sender reputation.

Let's dive in—and unlock the full potential of your email marketing strategy.

Why Email Engagement Matters More Than Ever

Engagement is the heartbeat of email marketing. It's not just about sending emails—it's about what happens next. Did they open it? Did they click through? Did they respond or convert?

Here's why boosting engagement is critical:

- **Increased deliverability:** Email providers prioritize messages with strong engagement, meaning your future emails are less likely to land in spam.

- **Stronger relationships:** Engaged clients are more likely to become repeat buyers, refer your services, and trust your recommendations.

- **Higher ROI:** Email consistently returns $36 for every $1 spent—but only if people engage with your campaigns.

The Power of Email List Hygiene

Before you think about subject lines or visuals, the foundation is your email list. Sending emails to unverified or uninterested recipients is like pouring water into a leaky bucket—it wastes resources and damages your brand reputation.

What is Email List Hygiene?

List hygiene refers to the regular process of verifying and cleaning your contact list to remove:

- Invalid email addresses

- Fake or temporary accounts

- Inactive subscribers

- Duplicate entries

Why It Matters?

- **Improves Deliverability:** Email providers penalize senders with high bounce rates. A clean list improves sender reputation and keeps you in the inbox.

- **Reduces Spam Complaints:** Engaged contacts are less likely to mark your emails as spam.

- **Boosts Campaign Metrics:** Open and click rates increase when your list consists of real, interested people.

Signs Your List Needs Cleaning

- Increasing bounce rates

- Lower open and click rates over time

- Higher spam complaints

- Poor conversion metrics

Using Email Verification Tools for Better Accuracy

Email verification tools help you confirm that the addresses in your list are:

- Active
- Properly formatted
- Associated with real domains
- Not blacklisted or risky

Benefits of Email Verification Tools

1. Reduce Bounce Rates: By filtering out invalid addresses, you protect your sender score and ensure your emails are delivered.

2. Save on Costs: Many email platforms charge based on subscriber count. Why pay for dead weight?

3. Improve Accuracy: Focus on reaching people who are more likely to open, read, and respond to your emails.

Top Features to Look For

- Real-time verification
- Syntax and domain checking
- Catch-all detection
- Integration with your CRM or email platform
- GDPR compliance

Email Verification Services for Enhanced Deliverability

Unlike tools that simply scan for active addresses, full-service email verification platforms often provide more comprehensive support, such as:

- Batch verification for large lists
- Risk scoring
- Spam trap detection
- API access for automated workflows

Case Study Example

A SaaS company noticed a 22% drop in email performance over three months. After using an email verification service, they discovered nearly 18% of their contacts were invalid or expired. Cleaning the list restored their open rates and boosted conversions by 15% in the following campaign.

Best Practices When Using Verification Services

- Verify your list at least once a quarter
- Always verify before importing contacts from third-party sources or events
- Combine verification with re-engagement campaigns to clean inactive users

Choosing the Best Email Verification Tool for Your Business

Not all tools are created equal. Here's what to consider when making a choice:

1. Real-Time Verification

Great for sign-up forms or landing pages. Prevent fake emails from ever entering your list.

2. Bulk Verification

Essential for periodic list cleaning. Choose a tool that allows batch uploads and exports verified results quickly.

3..Ease of Integration

Ensure the tool connects smoothly with your existing systems—whether it's Mailchimp, HubSpot, Klaviyo, or your CRM.

4. Support and Scalability

You need responsive support, especially when dealing with large lists or technical issues. As your business grows, the tool should scale with you.

5. Pricing Transparency

Make sure there are no hidden fees. Most platforms charge per 1,000 or 10,000 emails verified.

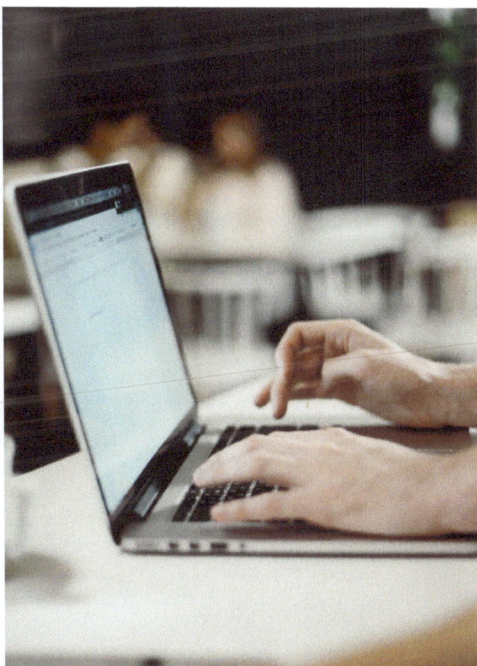

Crafting Engaging and Personalized Content

Now that your list is clean and verified, it's time to focus on the content. Personalization and segmentation go beyond using someone's name—they're about relevance.

Why Personalization Works

- Personalized emails generate 6x higher transaction rates

- Emails with tailored content have higher open and click-through rates

- 80% of consumers are more likely to do business with a company that offers personalized experiences

How to Personalize Effectively

- Use behavior-based triggers: past purchases, pages viewed, time on site

- Send birthday or anniversary emails

- Tailor content based on geography, demographics, or interests

Dynamic Content in Action

An e-commerce store can show winter boots to customers in colder climates, while promoting sandals to users in warmer regions—all in the same email template.

The Role of Segmentation in Client Engagement

Segmentation is the practice of dividing your audience into groups based on specific criteria.

Common Segmentation Criteria

- Purchase behavior

- Email engagement (opens/clicks)

- Industry or job role

- Geographic location

- Lifecycle stage (lead, client, repeat customer)

Segmenting for Better Engagement

- Send a thank-you sequence to recent purchasers

- Re-engage users who haven't opened in 90 days

- Upsell premium services to frequent users

Utilizing A/B Testing to Optimize Campaign Performance

Email marketing shouldn't be guesswork. A/B testing empowers you to make decisions based on data, not assumptions.

What to Test

- Subject lines

- Preheader text

- CTA placement and wording

- Layout and design

- Time and day of sending

How to Run Effective Tests

1. Test one variable at a time

2. Ensure your sample size is large enough

3. Use statistically significant results to inform decisions

4. Apply winning variations to future campaigns

Quick Example

An online retailer tested two subject lines:

- A: "Get 20% Off Today"

- B: "Your Loyalty Deserves a Reward—20% Off Inside!"

Result: Version B increased opens by 27% and clicks by 18%.

Timing and Frequency: Finding the Sweet Spot

Even the best emails fall flat if they're sent at the wrong time or too often.

Best Practices

- Test different days and times (e.g., Tuesdays at 10 AM vs. Fridays at 3 PM)

- Respect your audience's attention—avoid over-sending

- Let subscribers choose preferences (weekly, biweekly, monthly updates)

Timing Tools

Use AI-powered platforms that analyze engagement trends and send emails at the optimal time for each subscriber.

Re-engaging Inactive Subscribers

Not everyone stays engaged forever. Instead of removing them immediately, give them a reason to reconnect.

Re-engagement Campaign Ideas

- "We Miss You" emails with special offers

- Feedback requests ("Why haven't you opened our emails?")

- Reminders of what they signed up for

Re-engagement Best Practices

- Limit to 2–3 attempts

- Be clear and direct

- Remove those who don't engage—this helps with list health

Building Trust Through Email

Email isn't just for selling—it's a trust-building channel. Every interaction shapes how clients see your brand.

Strategies to Build Trust

- Be consistent with your tone and values

- Deliver on your promises

- Use double opt-in for signup confirmation

- Include a visible unsubscribe link

Transparency builds loyalty. Respect earns engagement.

Metrics That Matter: Measuring Engagement

To refine your strategy, track meaningful metrics:

Key Engagement Metrics

- Open rate: Measures subject line effectiveness

- Click-through rate (CTR): Indicates content relevance

- Conversion rate: Measures email ROI

- Bounce rate: Tracks email list quality

- Unsubscribe rate: Reveals dissatisfaction or over-sending

Use dashboards or integrations to track performance over time and tie it back to campaign goals.

Frequently Asked Questions (FAQs)

1. How would email verification impact my email marketing campaign?

It dramatically improves deliverability by ensuring you're only sending to valid email addresses, reducing bounce rates and increasing engagement.

2. What is the difference between an email verification tool and service?

A tool often verifies emails in real time during sign-up. A service usually offers more extensive features like bulk verification, spam trap detection, and integration capabilities.

3. What are the best features of email verification tools for small businesses?

Look for affordability, ease of use, CRM/email integration, and fast batch processing. Scalability is also important as your list grows.

4. How often should I clean my email list?

Quarterly is ideal for most businesses, though monthly may be better for larger or high-volume lists.

5. What's more important: email design or content?

Both matter—but content wins in the long run. Clear, value-driven messaging builds relationships; great design supports it.

Final Thoughts: Elevating Your Email Strategy

Maximizing client engagement isn't just about eye-catching templates or witty subject lines. It goes much deeper than that. True engagement stems from a strategic, holistic approach that prioritizes both the health of your email list and the quality of your content. This means regularly cleaning your list to remove invalid or disengaged addresses, personalizing your messaging to resonate with individual recipients, and consistently testing and refining your approach based on performance data. At its core, successful email marketing is about being obsessively focused on delivering genuine value, not just promotions.

When you put email verification, thoughtful segmentation, and authentic personalization at the forefront of your strategy, you're doing more than sending out mass communications. You're cultivating meaningful, long-term relationships with your audience, one well-crafted message at a time. Every email becomes an opportunity to build trust and credibility. So, before your next campaign goes live, take a moment to reflect: Does this email truly serve my audience as much as it serves my goals? Because when you lead with value and intent, engagement isn't just a metric. It's a natural outcome.

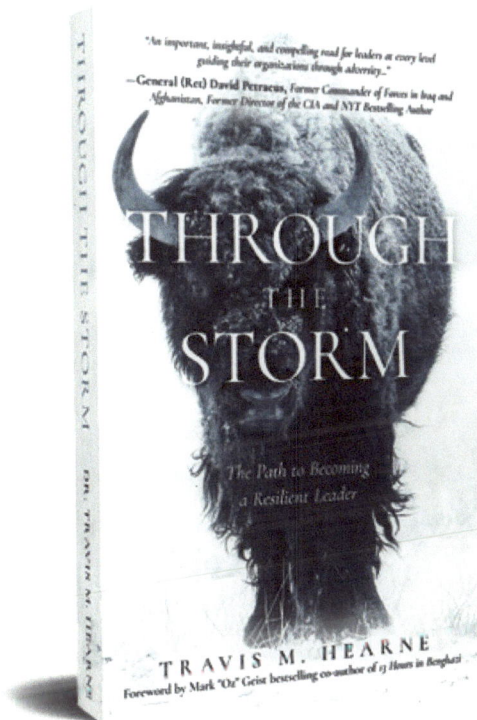

The Future of Mobile Connectivity with eSIM Technology

The demand for streamlined, flexible, and secure mobile connectivity has never been more urgent. As businesses expand globally, remote work becomes standard, and consumers rely on multiple connected devices throughout their day, the limitations of traditional SIM cards are becoming increasingly clear. These physical chips, while reliable in the past, lack the adaptability needed to keep pace with a rapidly evolving digital ecosystem. The modern world calls for a solution that offers not just connectivity, but smart connectivity—dynamic, programmable, and easy to manage across devices and borders.

That's where eSIM (embedded SIM) technology comes in. Unlike its physical predecessor, eSIM is built directly into a device's hardware, allowing users to activate a mobile network without the need to insert a physical card. This opens the door to a new level of flexibility—users can switch carriers, manage plans remotely, and stay connected wherever they are, all with minimal friction. As the backbone for innovations in 5G and the Internet of Things (IoT), eSIM is reshaping industries by enabling scalable, secure, and remote device provisioning. From smartphones and smartwatches to connected cars and industrial sensors, eSIM isn't just an upgrade. It's a transformation in how we connect and communicate.

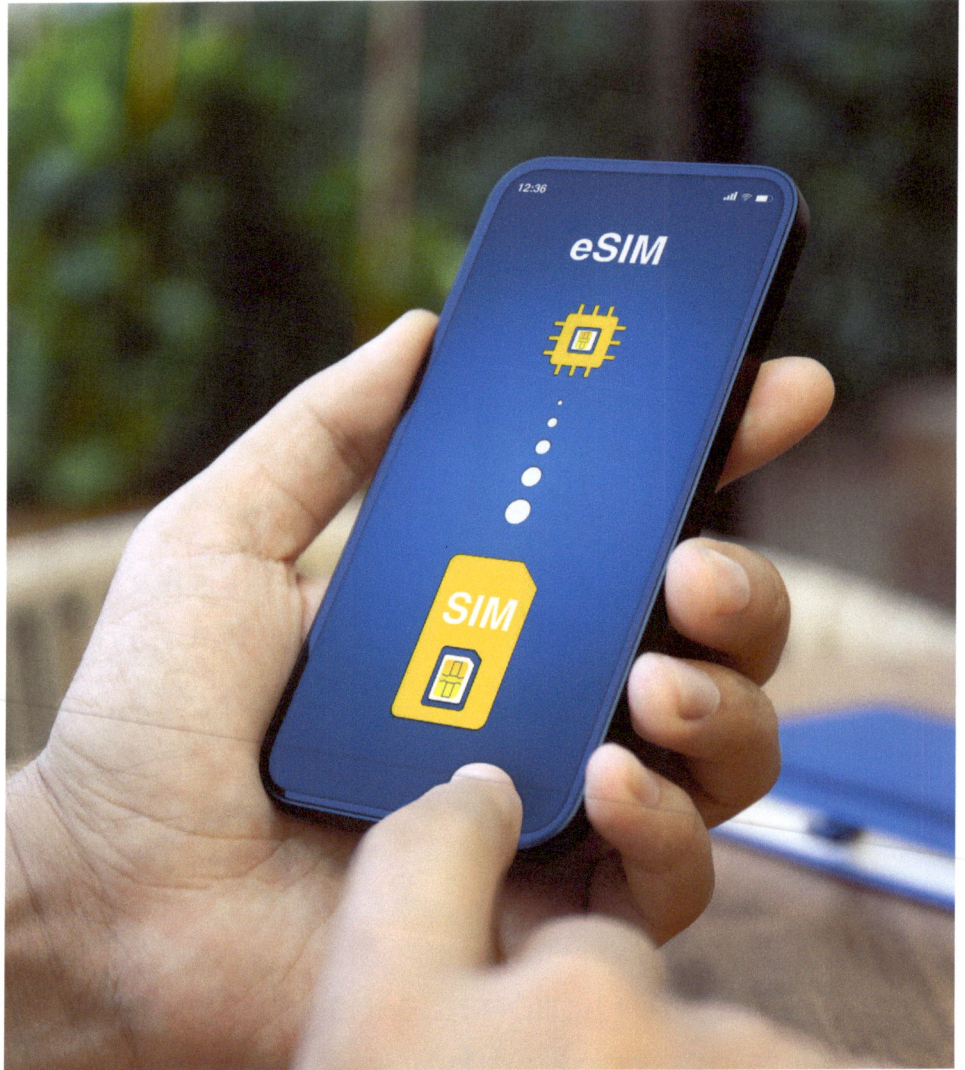

eSIM: The Game Changer in Mobile Connectivity

Unlike the traditional plastic SIM card that can be removed and swapped between devices, an eSIM is embedded directly into the device's hardware. It's rewritable, remotely programmable, and capable of holding multiple mobile network profiles. This innovation transforms the experience of connectivity by giving users more control and flexibility.

For **frequent travelers**, **remote workers**, and **digital nomads**, eSIM eliminates the need to hunt for a local SIM card or juggle physical SIMs. Instead, users can instantly activate local plans or switch between carriers from their device settings.

Example in Action

Let's say you're traveling from the U.S. to Japan for a business trip. Instead of arriving and searching for a kiosk that sells SIM cards, you could activate a Japanese data plan on your eSIM before you land. This not only saves time and effort—it avoids roaming fees and ensures you're connected the moment you step off the plane.

Enhanced Security and Simplified Management

Security remains one of the primary concerns for mobile users and businesses alike. eSIM technology introduces new layers of protection compared to traditional SIMs.

Built-In Protection

Since eSIMs are built into the device, they cannot be physically stolen or swapped without access to the device itself. This makes them ideal for use in corporate settings where device security is critical.

Additionally, **eSIM profiles can be updated or deactivated remotely**, providing IT teams with centralized control over distributed devices. This is particularly helpful in industries such as healthcare, logistics, and finance, where data protection is non-negotiable.

Enterprise Use Cases

For businesses managing thousands of devices, such as in fleet management or smart agriculture, eSIM allows IT administrators to:

- Provision or switch data plans without retrieving the device

- Remotely lock or wipe profiles in the event of theft

- Monitor usage and compliance more efficiently

This lowers operational costs and reduces device downtime.

Driving the IoT Revolution

IoT is rapidly transforming industries—smart thermostats, wearable health monitors, connected cars, industrial

These devices demand consistent, global connectivity.

Why eSIM is Perfect for IoT

1. Remote Provisioning: Devices don't need to be touched or physically modified to change their carrier.

2. Compact Design: eSIMs take up less space, which is crucial for compact or embedded devices.

3. Scalability: Devices can be deployed and managed anywhere in the world without SIM logistics.

Real-World Impact

- Smart Cities: eSIM enables sensors to communicate across cities for waste management, energy use, and public safety.

- Automotive: Vehicles with embedded eSIMs can access live traffic updates, stream media, and perform over-the-air (OTA) updates without needing a traditional SIM.

- Wearables: Smartwatches and fitness trackers benefit from reduced size and better integration with cellular networks.

Comparison Table: Traditional SIM vs. eSIM

Feature	Traditional SIM	eSIM
Physical Card Requirement	Required	Not Required
Switching Carriers	Involved physical SIM change	Done digitally via settings
Security	Vulnerable to loss/theft	More secure, embedded in a device
Multiple Profiles	Requires multiple SIMs	Multiple profiles on one eSIM
IoT Device Management	Challenging, physical swaps	Simplified, remote management
Global Deployment	Require local SIMs	Seamless with remote provisioning

Impact on the Telecom Industry

The introduction of eSIM is not just a consumer upgrade. It represents a strategic challenge and opportunity for telecom companies worldwide.

Disrupting the Carrier Lock-In Model

Historically, telecom providers controlled SIM distribution and used it to maintain customer contracts. eSIM breaks this dependency. Users can:

- Switch carriers directly from their phone

- Try short-term plans on the go

- Opt for carriers offering better performance or value

This forces telecom providers to focus on **experience-driven loyalty**, offering competitive pricing, better customer service, and innovative plans to retain users.

Creating New Business Models

Carriers can no longer rely solely on long-term lock-ins. With eSIM, the following business models are emerging:

- **On-demand data plans** for travelers or event attendees

- **Flexible, pay-as-you-go subscriptions** with no long-term commitment

- **Integrated device + data bundles** for wearables, tablets, and smart home devices

eSIM makes it easier for telecoms to support partnerships with third-party device makers, allowing direct activation of carrier services during device setup.

Preparing for the 5G Era

As 5G expands globally, eSIM is becoming more relevant and indispensable.

The Role of eSIM in 5G

5G networks promise:
- Lightning-fast speeds

- Ultra-low latency

- Support for massive IoT deployments

But traditional SIM management can't keep up with the dynamic needs of 5G environments. eSIM simplifies:

- Connecting to the fastest local 5G network

- Switching carriers in case of outages

- Scaling IoT deployments quickly and securely

Example Use Case

An autonomous vehicle fleet in a smart city requires uninterrupted 5G connectivity to communicate with traffic systems. eSIM enables seamless carrier switching based on location, network quality, or usage needs. All in real time.

Global Adoption Trends

Countries around the world are embracing eSIM, though adoption rates vary.

Leading the Charge

- **United States:** Major carriers like Verizon, AT&T, and T-Mobile offer eSIM support for both consumers and enterprises.

- **Europe:** eSIM adoption is widespread in countries like Germany, UK, and France, driven by tech-savvy consumers and robust 5G rollout.

- **Asia-Pacific**: Japan, South Korea, and Australia are accelerating eSIM-enabled device availability and infrastructure.

Challenges in Emerging Markets

- Slower rollout of supporting infrastructure

- Limited eSIM-compatible devices

- Regulatory hurdles around carrier switching

As the benefits become clearer, pressure will mount for carriers in emerging markets to modernize and support eSIM standards.

Environmental and Economic Impact

eSIM technology isn't just about connectivity. It also supports sustainability and cost savings.

Environmental Benefits

- Reduces plastic waste from millions of discarded SIM cards

- Minimizes logistics involved in SIM production and shipping

- Decreases carbon footprint by enabling remote provisioning

Economic Benefits

- Cuts costs related to logistics, warehousing, and retail distribution

- Reduces need for physical stores and in-person SIM swaps

- Enables smaller, lighter device designs (especially useful in wearables and IoT)

Challenges and Considerations

While eSIM is a breakthrough, it's not without its challenges.

1. Device Compatibility

Many newer smartphones, tablets, and wearables support eSIM but older devices do not. This slows adoption, especially in price-sensitive markets.

2. Carrier Support

While the number of eSIM-supporting carriers is growing, some still resist due to fears of customer churn. Until global support becomes standardized, some users may face compatibility issues.

3. Consumer Awareness

Many people are unaware of what eSIM is or how to use it. Activating and switching eSIM profiles can seem complicated to non-tech-savvy users.

What's needed?

- Better user education
- Simplified interfaces
- More marketing around benefits

eSIM and Privacy

Privacy is a growing concern in a connected world. eSIM's centralized management opens doors for better oversight but also new risks if mismanaged.

Benefits

- Device tracking becomes harder for thieves
- Data breaches from lost SIM cards are reduced
- Personal info can be wiped remotely

Risks

- Centralized management could be exploited if security is compromised
- Users must trust carriers and manufacturers to safeguard eSIM data

Looking Ahead: Innovations on the Horizon

eSIM is paving the way for even more advanced connectivity models.

iSIM (Integrated SIM)

The next evolution is **iSIM**, which integrates SIM functionality into the device's main processor. This takes up even less space and uses less power, ideal for ultra-small devices and smart sensors.

Multi-IMSI Profiles

New technology may allow devices to access multiple carrier profiles simultaneously, choosing the best option based on pricing, signal strength, or location.

Embracing the Future of Connectivity

eSIM is not just a tech upgrade—it's a shift in how people, businesses, and systems stay connected. It offers:

- More control for users

- Better efficiency for enterprises

- Increased flexibility for developers and manufacturers

As 5G, IoT, and global mobility continue to expand, eSIM will be at the heart of this transformation.

What You Can Do

- Consumers: Explore eSIM-compatible devices, especially if you travel often or use multiple lines.

- Businesses: Assess eSIM for device fleets, IoT deployments, or global workforce mobility.

- Developers: Build apps and platforms that support eSIM management and automation.

Frequently Asked Questions

1. Will eSIM technology work with all mobile carriers?

No, not all carriers currently support eSIM, but adoption is increasing globally. Always check with your provider before switching.

2. Can I use multiple carriers on a single device with eSIM?

Yes, many eSIM-enabled devices allow multiple profiles, making it easy to switch between networks without changing SIM cards.

3. How secure is eSIM compared to traditional SIM cards?

eSIM is generally more secure. It cannot be physically stolen or removed and offers enhanced remote management features.

4. What devices support eSIM?

Most flagship smartphones from Apple, Samsung, and Google support eSIM, as do many tablets, laptops, wearables, and IoT devices.

5. How do I activate an eSIM?

You typically scan a QR code provided by your carrier or download a carrier profile directly to your device via settings.

Conclusion

eSIM technology is redefining the future of mobile connectivity. From simplifying international travel to transforming enterprise device management and fueling the rise of the Internet of Things, its impact is profound and far-reaching.

As adoption accelerates and technology evolves, eSIM will become the new norm—not just a convenience, but a necessity in a hyper-connected world.

Whether you're a frequent traveler, a tech-forward business, or a curious consumer—embracing eSIM now positions you at the forefront of digital innovation.

The future is flexible. The future is remote. The future is eSIM.

JOIN
Achieve Systems

BECOME AN ACHIEVE SYSTEMS MEMBER TODAY!

Education
We help you get the tools to create a thriving business! It's turnkey, you can start NOW!

Marketing
We provide marketing guidelines but also plug you into our conferences, events and database

Community
We have a thriving community of entrepreneurs and business owners for you to collaborate, refer and partner with to grow and up-level your business!

WE WORK WITH ENTREPRENEURS, BUSINESS OWNERS, SPEAKERS & LEADERS!

CONTACT US OR REGISTER HERE: www.AchieveSystemsPro.com

How AI is Changing the Dynamics of Restaurant Customer Service

Imagine stepping into your favorite restaurant not just for the food, but for the experience. The host greets you by name. Your favorite dish is already queued up based on your last visit. There's no awkward wait time, no order mix-ups, no flagging down a server. Instead, what greets you is a seamless, efficient, and highly personalized experience. Sound like science fiction? Think again. This is the reality being shaped by artificial intelligence (AI), and it's unfolding in restaurants around the world right now.

Over the past few years, AI has evolved from a buzzword into a powerful tool that's actively transforming the restaurant landscape. With today's customers demanding faster service, tailored recommendations, and smoother interactions, restaurants are leaning into AI not just to stay competitive, but to stay relevant. AI is no longer a futuristic luxury; it's rapidly becoming the foundation of modern hospitality.

Whether it's self-service kiosks that remember your usual order, voice-activated assistants that let you modify dishes on the fly, or sophisticated algorithms that forecast inventory and optimize staff schedules, AI is quietly but radically enhancing every touchpoint of the dining experience. And this isn't just a fleeting trend—the global market for food robotics and AI in hospitality is expected to skyrocket, projected to reach tens of billions of dollars by 2030.

In this article, we'll break down how AI is redefining restaurant customer service from front-of-house interactions to back-of- kitchen operations. You'll learn how smart tech is improving accuracy, reducing waste, boosting speed, and creating a dining journey that feels more human, not less. Whether you're a seasoned restaurateur looking to innovate, or a tech-savvy foodie curious about what's cooking behind the scenes, buckle up. We're diving into a smarter, faster, and more intuitive era of dining—served up with a side of code.

AI-Driven Personalization in Dining Experiences

Personalization has always been a hallmark of great service. But with AI, personalization becomes smarter, scalable, and real-time.

How AI Delivers Personalized Experiences

Modern AI systems can analyze your dining preferences, previous orders, dietary restrictions, and even the time of day you usually dine. Based on this data, restaurants can:

- Suggest personalized menu items

- Offer targeted discounts

- Recommend complementary sides or drinks

For example, if you frequently order plant-based meals, the restaurant's AI system can automatically suggest new vegan options or alert you to an upcoming plant-based promotion.

Real-World Application

Domino's uses AI to offer "Easy Order" based on past behavior. Starbucks leverages its AI-driven "Deep Brew" platform to tailor menu boards, app suggestions, and marketing messages to individual customers.

This level of customization enhances customer satisfaction and boosts loyalty, because customers feel recognized and understood.

Enhanced Customer Interaction with AI

In a world where speed and convenience matter, AI is revolutionizing how customers interact with restaurants.

Chatbots and Virtual Assistants

AI chatbots are handling a wide range of tasks:

- Booking reservations

- Answering frequently asked questions

- Recommending dishes

- Offering real-time support

Unlike human staff, chatbots are available 24/7, offer consistent responses, and can handle multiple queries at once.

Multilingual Support

Some AI-powered systems can even interact in multiple languages—an advantage for restaurants in multicultural or tourist-heavy areas. This inclusivity improves accessibility and enhances the guest experience.

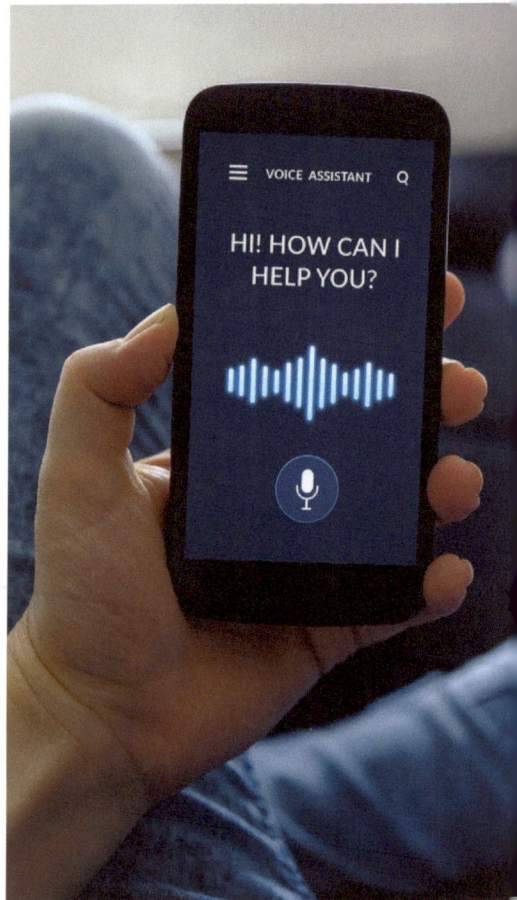

Smart Voice Ordering

AI voice assistants like those used in drive-thrus or phone-in orders can take accurate orders quickly, reducing errors and improving efficiency. In 2023, Wendy's and Google Cloud partnered to deploy voice AI in drive-thrus—a move that's setting the stage for others to follow.

Operational Efficiency Through AI

AI doesn't just impact the front of the house—it revolutionizes how restaurants are run behind the scenes.

Labor Optimization

AI forecasts customer demand based on weather, time, seasonality, and special events. This helps restaurant managers:

- Schedule the right number of staff
- Minimize overtime and idle labor
- Enhance service during peak hours

Inventory and Waste Reduction

By analyzing historical sales and external factors (like local events or weather forecasts), AI predicts which ingredients will be needed. This means:

- Less spoilage
- Fewer stockouts
- Better vendor coordination

Chipotle, for example, uses AI to monitor ingredient consumption in real time, helping to minimize waste while keeping popular items in stock.

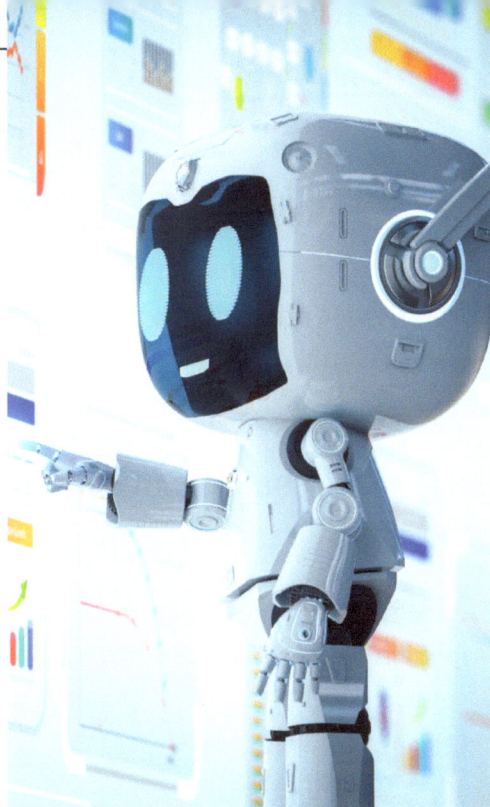

Predictive Maintenance

AI also keeps tabs on kitchen appliances. It can predict when an oven might fail or a refrigerator's temperature may fluctuate—allowing proactive maintenance and reducing costly downtime.

AI-Enhanced Customer Feedback Mechanisms

Feedback is critical in any service industry, and AI is changing how it's collected, processed, and used.

Real-Time Sentiment Analysis

AI tools can monitor reviews, social media posts, and survey responses. By analyzing sentiment, restaurants get a pulse on customer satisfaction, identifying issues before they escalate.

Automated Feedback Collection

Instead of waiting for guests to fill out lengthy forms, AI-driven tools can:

- Send short post-dining surveys
- Collect star ratings
- Prompt guests for voice feedback

All of this data can then be categorized into actionable insights—helping management prioritize improvements.

Smart Response Systems

AI can even handle responses to online reviews thanking happy customers, escalating complaints, and suggesting future promotions. This consistent follow-up reinforces the customer's voice and builds brand loyalty.

Seamless Integration Across All Touchpoints

The true power of AI lies in its ability to work across all areas of the restaurant business in harmony.

Unified Customer Profiles

When data from POS systems, loyalty apps, online orders, and in-person interactions are synced, AI can create comprehensive customer profiles. These insights drive:

- Menu design

- Promotions

- Loyalty rewards

- Staff training

Predictive Marketing

By analyzing patterns, AI can determine when a customer is likely to return and offer timely promotions like a half-off pizza coupon before their usual Friday night order.

Omnichannel Integration

Whether you're ordering from a kiosk, app, or website, AI ensures a consistent experience across platforms. It recognizes your preferences and applies them wherever you interact with the brand.

AI in Action: Smart Kitchens and Robotics

AI isn't just in the software. It's physically in the kitchen too.

Kitchen Automation

Robots powered by AI can:

- Flip burgers

- Dispense drinks

- Cook pasta

- Plate meals with precision

Miso Robotics' "Flippy" is a robotic arm that works fry stations in fast food restaurants, improving safety and speed.

Quality Control

AI-powered cameras in restaurant kitchens monitor how dishes are plated. They analyze food presentation in real time to ensure it aligns with brand standards. This helps maintain consistency and visual appeal across every order. Even during the busiest rush, quality stays high thanks to automated oversight.

Comparing Traditional vs. AI-Powered Restaurant Service

Here's a comparison of how AI stacks up against traditional service:

Feature	Traditional Service	AI-Powered Service
Menu Suggestions	Static menu	Personalized recommendations
Order Handling	Human error prone	Automated & accurate
Staffing	Manual scheduling	Predictive staffing
Customer Feedback	Manual reviews	Real-time sentiment analysis
Inventory	Manual tracking	Predictive inventory management
Customer Interaction	In-person only	24/7 chatbots & voice AI

The differences are clear: AI leads to faster, smarter, and more efficient restaurant service at nearly every touchpoint.

Challenges and Concerns of AI in Restaurants

While AI offers undeniable benefits, it also presents challenges that must be addressed:

1. Data Privacy

AI systems rely on customer data to provide personalized experiences. Ensuring that data is stored securely and used ethically is essential to maintain customer trust.

2. Technology Costs

AI solutions—especially robotics and integrated

Restaurants must weigh upfront costs against long-term gains like labor savings and improved efficiency.

3. Learning Curve for Staff

Integrating AI requires employee training. Teams must learn how to work with chatbots, use AI-powered analytics, and maintain automated systems.

4. Loss of Human Touch

A common concern is that AI could strip restaurants of their personal charm. However, successful restaurants are using AI to complement—not replace—human service.

Future Trends in AI and Restaurant Customer Service

As AI technology matures, here's what we can expect next:

1. Emotion AI

New tools will be able to detect customer emotions through voice tone or facial

expressions. Restaurants may tailor experiences based on mood.

2. Augmented Reality Menus

AI-powered AR will allow diners to visualize meals before ordering, reducing decision fatigue and increasing upsells.

3. Hyper-Personalized Loyalty Programs

AI will customize rewards based on each customer's unique behavior—offering coffee discounts to frequent caffeine lovers or free dessert to birthday diners.

4. Voice Commerce

Voice assistants like Alexa or Google Assistant may soon handle food orders entirely by voice—no screen needed.

5. AI-Driven Sustainability

AI will help restaurants reduce their environmental footprint by optimizing energy use, minimizing waste,

Case Study: How McDonald's is Using AI to Revolutionize Fast Food

McDonald's, the world's largest fast-food chain, has embraced artificial intelligence as a key driver of innovation and customer experience. In 2019, the company made headlines by acquiring Dynamic Yield, an AI-powered personalization platform. This move allowed McDonald's to transform its drive-thru experience with dynamic menus that adapt in real-time based on factors like the weather, time of day, local traffic patterns, and even a customer's previous order history. For example, on a hot day, the system might highlight cold drinks or ice cream, while during breakfast hours, it could prioritize coffee and egg-based options. This smart personalization not only speeds up decision-making for customers but also increases upsell opportunities—helping boost sales without disrupting the flow.

By investing heavily in AI across multiple touchpoints, from ordering to operations, McDonald's is setting the standard for AI adoption in quick-service restaurants. Their tech-forward approach not only enhances efficiency but also reflects a larger trend in the food industry: using smart technology to deliver faster, more personalized, and ultimately better customer experiences.

Frequently Asked Questions (FAQs)

1. How does AI impact the quality of customer service in restaurants?

AI enhances service by enabling personalization, reducing wait times, streamlining order accuracy, and improving guest feedback analysis.

2. What are the primary concerns regarding the use of AI in restaurant customer service?

Data privacy, job displacement fears, upfront investment, and potential loss of personal touch are top concerns.

3. How can restaurants ensure AI enhances—rather than replaces—human service?

By using AI to handle repetitive tasks, staff are freed up to focus on personalized, face-to-face interactions that build loyalty and create memorable experiences.

4. What types of AI are most commonly used in restaurants?

Chatbots, voice assistants, facial recognition, predictive analytics, sentiment analysis tools, and inventory management systems.

5. How does AI help restaurants manage their inventory?

AI forecasts demand by analyzing historical sales, trends, and real-time data—ensuring stock of high-demand items while reducing waste.

6. Is AI implementation in restaurants affordable for small businesses?

Yes. AI tools like chatbots and cloud analytics are now accessible to smaller restaurants. Many offer flexible pricing, so businesses can start small and scale up.

Final Thoughts: A Recipe for the Future

AI is not replacing hospitality—it's redefining it. The best restaurant experiences still come from thoughtful service, but AI helps make those moments more frequent, more consistent, and more memorable.

By automating routine tasks and providing deeper insights, AI gives restaurant teams more time to do what they do best: delight customers.

Restaurants that balance smart automation with human warmth will be the ones that thrive. Whether you're a small local café or a global chain, AI offers a menu full of possibilities to serve better, smarter, and more meaningfully.

MICROCASTING

Supercharge Your Business!

Do you want to find new ways to add additional income to your coaching ,consulting, or content creation business?

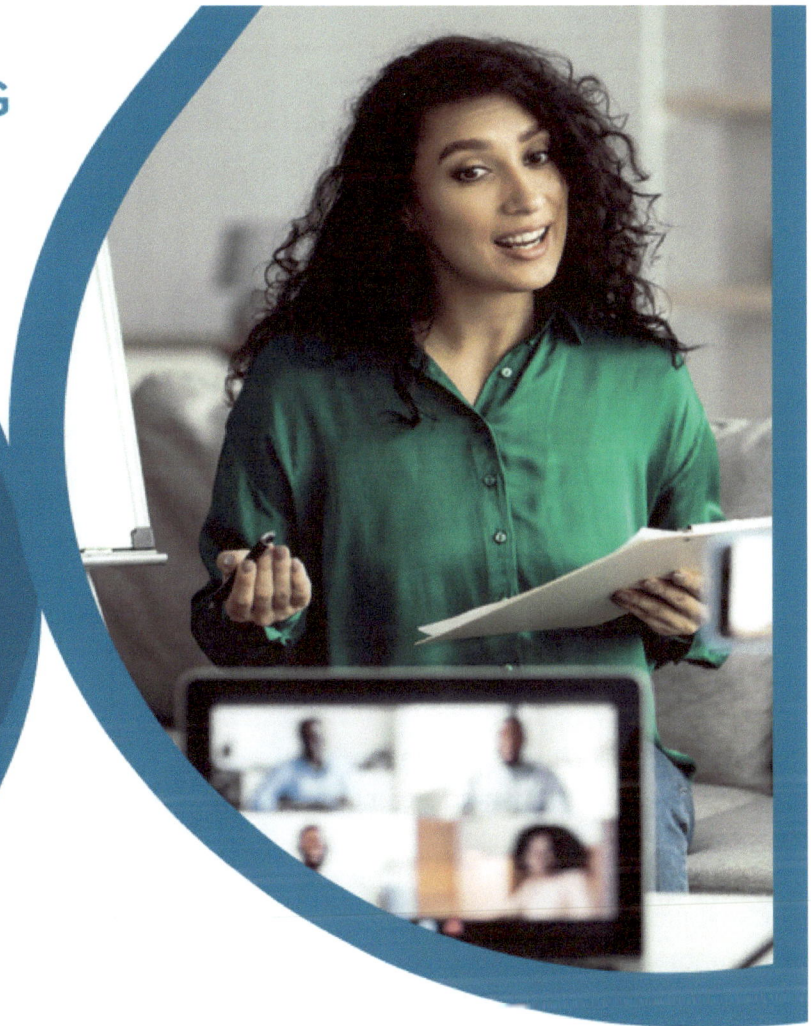

eLearning Portals by Microcasting is specifically designed for Coaches, Consultants, and Course Creators to engage your customers, establish yourself as a thought leader, and grow your revenues.

Here are just a few things you can do with **Microcasting**:

- ⊘ **Start selling** your courses and programs.
- ⊘ Create a **paid membership site** to grow your revenues.
- ⊘ Build a free membership site to **increase lead gen**.
- ⊘ Easily **integrate eLearning** into your marketing website.
- ⊘ Create **individualized customer portals** .
- ⊘ And so much more...

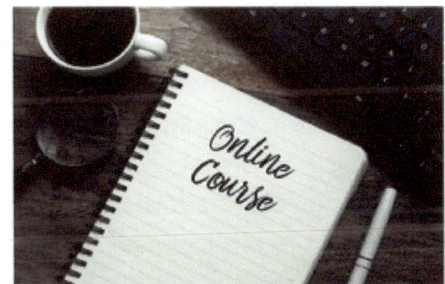

Microcasting is an all-in-one online learning platform that makes it easy for course creators to design, manage, and market their courses. With its personalized eLearning experience, you can keep your current customers engaged with your business, generating more upsells and higher renewal rates. Create courses quickly and effortlessly - all with the help of Microcasting!

Try Microcasting today and start transforming your business!

Request a demo - email us at ✉ info@microcasting.com **OR VISIT** 🌐 www.elearning-portals.com

5 Tips on Finding the Best Loans for Businesses in Specific Industries

Numerous businesses across a wide range of industries depend on loan programs to maintain and grow their operations. Whether it's to fuel expansion plans, cover seasonal dips in revenue, invest in new equipment, manage day-to-day cash flow, or seize time-sensitive opportunities, access to the right financing can be a game-changer. From established corporations to scrappy startups, the ability to secure the right type of funding often plays a pivotal role in shaping a company's success and long-term viability.

However, if you operate within a specific industry, be it healthcare, retail, manufacturing, construction, travel and hospitality, or newer sectors like clean energy or tech startups, you'll soon realize that there's no one-size-fits-all loan solution. Each sector has its own set of operating challenges, financial rhythms, regulatory landscapes, and growth patterns. What works for a fast-scaling software company may not suit a medical practice or a seasonal tourism business.

These industry-specific nuances mean that choosing the right loan program isn't just a financial decision. It's a strategic one.

Understanding the lending landscape through the lens of your industry allows you to identify financing that complements your cash flow cycles, supports your business goals, and avoids unnecessary costs or constraints. The right loan should empower your business, not restrict it.

Still, with so many financing options out there—from traditional bank loans and SBA programs to revenue-based financing, equipment leasing, and newer fintech offerings—navigating the loan market can feel like wading through a maze. The variety is great, but it can also be overwhelming, especially if you're unsure what to prioritize or how to compare your choices.

To help simplify the process and make your decision-making more strategic, we've put together an expanded guide. Inside, you'll find five key tips to help you identify the best loan programs for your specific industry. These insights are designed to take the guesswork out of the search and include practical steps, real-world examples, and industry-aligned strategies—so you can make informed financing decisions with confidence.

Tip 1: Assess the Specific Needs of Your Industry

Before you even start comparing lenders or browsing loan types, it's critical to understand the financial ecosystem of your industry. Every business sector comes with different cash flow patterns, capital requirements, risk levels, and regulatory frameworks.

Why Industry-Specific Assessment Matters

- **Healthcare Providers** often require large upfront investments in expensive equipment but operate on delayed payments from insurance providers.

- **Retail Businesses** experience seasonal fluctuations, needing short-term capital for inventory stocking before peak seasons.

- **Manufacturing Companies** typically require heavy machinery, large facilities, and bulk material purchases, demanding long-term, substantial financing.

- **Travel and Hospitality** industries may need working capital loans to survive off-peak seasons and invest heavily during peak seasons.

Identifying your industry's financial cycles and operational demands helps you avoid mismatches between your loan obligations and your business realities.

How to Conduct a Needs Assessment

- **Review cash flow patterns** over several years if possible.

- **Forecast upcoming capital expenditures** (equipment, renovations, expansions).

- **Assess working capital needs** (inventory, seasonal staff, marketing pushes).

- **Outline long-term growth plans** and the capital needed to support them.

Understanding these factors allows you to choose loans with repayment structures and funding timelines that fit your specific circumstances.

Tip 2: Do Your Research on Industry-Specific Loan Programs

Once you've outlined your needs, the next logical step is researching loans that are designed with your industry in mind.

Benefits of Industry-Specific Loans

- Tailored repayment schedules (e.g., seasonal payments for farmers or retailers).

- Customized funding amounts aligned with typical industry expenses.

- Easier approval processes by lenders familiar with industry challenges.

- Specialized terms that consider the unique risks of your business sector..

Examples of Industry-Specific Loans

- **Healthcare Practice Loans:** Offered to doctors, dentists, and veterinarians, covering equipment, office setup, or practice acquisition.

- **Construction Loans:** Designed for contractors and developers, disbursed as needed for project phases rather than all upfront.

- **Retail Business Loans:** Short-term loans with flexible repayment for seasonal inventory buying or store expansions.

- **Hospitality Business Loans:** Help finance hotel renovations, marketing campaigns, or staffing during busy tourist seasons.

Lenders that offer these specialized programs usually have a deeper understanding of the operational and financial hurdles you face, resulting in a smoother application process and better loan structuring.

Tip 3: Explore Non-Industry-Specific Loan Types for Versatility

While industry-specific loans have clear advantages, don't overlook broader financing options that offer flexibility and can still align well with your business objectives.

Common Non-Industry-Specific Loans to Consider

- **Lines of Credit:** These provide on-demand access to funds up to a set limit, perfect for smoothing out cash flow fluctuations, covering emergency expenses, or capitalizing on sudden opportunities.

- **Equipment Financing:** While especially useful in manufacturing and construction, equipment loans can benefit any industry needing new tools, IT hardware, or vehicles.

- **Business Term Loans:** Ideal for a variety of purposes, from expanding to a new location to launching a new product line.

- **SBA (Small Business Administration) Loans:** Available to a wide range of industries, offering favorable terms like low-interest rates and longer repayment periods.

Real-World Example: Maya Flexi Loan (Philippines)

Maya Flexi Loan offers up to PHP2 million with flexible repayment terms and borrower-friendly fees. Businesses across sectors—whether they're selling online, operating physical shops, or offering professional services—can use these funds flexibly, allowing them to meet changing market demands.

Having non-industry-specific options in your toolkit ensures that if a niche loan doesn't suit you, you're not left without funding options.

Tip 4: Take Advantage of Government Loan Assistance Programs

Governments around the world offer specialized loan assistance programs designed to foster entrepreneurship, stimulate key industries, and support small to medium-sized enterprises (SMEs).

Advantages of Government Loans

- Lower interest rates than private loans.

- More extended repayment periods.

- Grace periods that delay your first payment.

- Less stringent eligibility requirements for SMEs.

- Risk-sharing guarantees that encourage lenders to approve more applications.

Popular Government Loan Programs

- **SBA 7(a) Loans (USA):** Ideal for businesses seeking working capital, equipment purchases, or real estate investments.

- **Pag-IBIG MSME Loan Program (Philippines):** Tailored for micro, small, and medium enterprises.

- **Start Up Loans Scheme (UK):** Offers unsecured personal loans and mentoring support for startups.

- **BDC Business Loans (Canada):** Helps SMEs with flexible financing for tech adoption, expansion, or purchasing inventory.

Even if you initially consider only private lenders, government-backed programs might offer better terms and a more forgiving structure—especially useful during economic downturns or if you're a newer business without an extensive credit history.

Pro Tip

Some programs cater specifically to businesses owned by women, minorities, or veterans, offering even more favorable terms or grant-loan hybrids. Always check for these niche opportunities.

Tip 5: Thoroughly Review Each Loan's Terms and Conditions

No matter how appealing a loan seems, you should never sign on the dotted line without carefully reviewing the fine print.

What to Watch Out For

- Interest Rates: Are they fixed or variable?

- Fees: Look for origination fees, prepayment penalties, and late payment charges.

- Collateral Requirements: Does the loan require putting up business or personal assets?

- Repayment Terms: Are payments monthly, quarterly, or seasonal?

- Covenants and Conditions: Are there restrictions on how you can use the funds?

- Balloon Payments: Is there a large lump-sum payment required at the end of the term?

Why Scrutinizing Terms Matters

A loan that looks affordable upfront can turn costly if hidden fees or inflexible terms create cash flow issues later. The best loan isn't just about getting the largest amount possible. It's about ensuring the loan supports your financial strategy without creating undue burden.

Take the time to compare offers side-by-side, or better yet, work with a financial advisor to decode complicated loan contracts.

Bonus Section: Mistakes to Avoid When Applying for a Business Loan

To ensure your loan application is successful, avoid these common pitfalls:

- **Failing to Prepare Accurate Financial Statements:** Incomplete or inaccurate financials can kill your application.

- **Applying for the Wrong Loan:** Mismatching loan type to business need leads to financial strain.

- **Ignoring Your Credit Score:** Poor credit can lead to higher interest rates or rejections. Work on improving your score before applying.

- **Overlooking Alternative Lenders:** Fintech companies and online lenders sometimes offer better rates and faster approvals than traditional banks.

- **Failing to Negotiate Terms:** Many business owners don't realize they can negotiate terms like repayment periods, interest rates, and fees.

- **Not Having a Clear Repayment Plan:** Lenders want to see how you'll pay the loan back. If you can't articulate a realistic plan for repayment, it raises red flags and can reduce your chances of approval—or land you with terms that strain your cash flow later.

Frequently Asked Questions (FAQs)

1. How do I know if an industry-specific loan is better than a general business loan?

If your industry has unique operating rhythms, large capital needs, or specific challenges, an industry-specific loan can offer better terms. Otherwise, flexible general loans may suffice.

2. Can startups qualify for industry-specific loans?

Some industry-specific loans are available to startups, but startups often have better chances with government-backed loans or flexible financing options like lines of credit.

3. What documents do I need to apply for a business loan?

Typically, you'll need financial statements, a business plan, tax returns, bank statements, and sometimes personal financial information, depending on the lender.

4. How important is my business credit score in loan approval?

Very important. Strong business credit can lower interest rates and secure better loan terms. Poor credit might limit your options or result in higher costs.

5. Are government loans easier to get than private business loans?

Not necessarily easier—they have different criteria. Government loans often require extensive documentation but offer better terms and lower costs for qualifying businesses.

6. How long does it typically take to get approved for a business loan?

Approval times depend on the lender and loan type. Banks may take weeks, while online lenders can approve in 24–72 hours. Don't forget to account for document prep and follow-up questions.

Conclusion: Choose the Right Loan, Choose the Right Future

Finding the best loan for your business isn't just about quick cash. It's about setting your company up for long-term success.

By assessing your industry's needs, researching niche programs, staying open to versatile loan options, leveraging government assistance, and carefully reviewing loan terms, you'll empower yourself to make smarter, more strategic financial decisions.

Remember: the right financing isn't a one-size-fits-all solution. It's a customized tool that should fit your goals, your growth plans, and your day-to-day operational realities. Businesses across industries, from healthcare to e-commerce, travel, and beyond, can use these tips to fuel success, gain competitive advantages, and thrive in increasingly complex marketplaces.

Unlocking the Potential: Solar Farms and Your Land's Value

The revolution in the energy sector is rapidly reshaping how property assets are evaluated across the real estate market. Among the most transformative developments is the rise of solar farm installations. Across various states in the United States, landowners are tapping into the financial opportunities of hosting solar energy projects.

Solar farms not only contribute to the clean energy transition but also offer landowners reliable long-term revenue, improved property value, and an enhanced investment profile. In this evolving landscape, those who adapt swiftly stand to benefit the most—financially, strategically, and environmentally.

In this detailed guide, we'll cover how solar farms impact your land's value, how to navigate the development process, how to assess your land's suitability, and how to future-proof your investment in the growing green economy.

The New Energy Frontier: Solar and Real Estate

The transition to clean energy is no longer a niche movement. According to the Solar Energy Industries Association (SEIA), solar power has experienced an average annual growth rate of 24% over the past decade. Federal and state incentives, corporate sustainability mandates, and sharp declines in the cost of solar technology are creating fertile ground for land-based solar developments.

Landowners today can think beyond traditional agriculture, residential development, or commercial leasing. By allowing a portion of their land to be used for a solar farm, they tap into a multi-decade revenue stream that is largely immune to economic downturns, commodity market volatility, or extreme weather, impacts common risks in traditional land uses.

As demand for renewable energy continues to rise, land leased for solar projects can also enhance a property's long-term value. Solar farms typically require minimal disturbance to the land itself, meaning that once the lease term ends, landowners often retain the flexibility to return to farming, redevelopment, or other uses, preserving future options while securing stable income today.

Navigating the Solar Farm Development Process

Step 1: Assess Your Land's Potential

Before contacting a developer, first, understand if your land is suitable. Developers typically seek:

- Minimum parcel sizes of 10–30 acres (the more, the better)

- Flat or gently sloping terrain

- Southern exposure to maximize sunlight capture

- Minimal shading from trees, buildings, or terrain

- Proximity to transmission lines and electrical substations

Not every property qualifies, but many that seem unlikely at first glance can be viable with the right planning.

Step 2: Research and Identify Developers

Compile a list of solar development companies operating in your state or region. Look for developers with:

- A strong track record of completed projects

- Transparent leasing practices

- Financial stability (critical for long-term commitments)

Ask for references from other landowners they've worked with.

Step 3: Get Legal Advice

Work with a real estate attorney experienced in renewable energy contracts. Key areas your lawyer should review include:

- Lease terms (length, escalators, rights)

- Tax implications

- Liability and insurance responsibilities

- Land restoration clauses

This guidance protects you from predatory or one-sided contract terms.

Step 4: Compare Offers

Do not settle for the first offer. Engage at least three developers to:

- Compare proposed lease payments

- Understand different operational plans

- Evaluate how each will handle decommissioning

Well-negotiated leases can result in annual payments ranging from $300 to $2,000 per acre, depending on location and project size.

Step 5: Understand Community Relations and Zoning

Solar farms typically need:

- Zoning approvals

- Conditional use permits

- Environmental impact studies

Developers usually manage these, but as the landowner, your local credibility can help smooth the process with community members and officials.

Evaluating Your Land for Solar Energy

Evaluating land suitability involves several important factors beyond just sun exposure.

Size and Configuration

- **Small Sites:** (10–30 acres) ideal for community solar projects.

- **Large Sites:** (50–500 acres) for utility-scale farms that sell directly to the power grid.

Odd-shaped parcels may still qualify if developers can maximize panel layout.

Terrain and Soil

- Prefer flat to gently sloping land.

- Soil must support the infrastructure but does not require high agricultural fertility.

Access and Logistics

- Developers need stable, all-weather road access for construction and maintenance.

- Proximity to towns or supply centers is a bonus.

Infrastructure Proximity

Being within a few miles of substations or high-voltage transmission lines significantly increases your land's attractiveness.

Impact on Real Estate Value

Hosting a solar farm can substantially enhance your land's value in several ways.

1. Steady Revenue Stream

A solar lease provides guaranteed income for 20–30 years, with annual escalators often tied to inflation indices.

2. Increased Property Valuation

Properties with solar leases sell at a premium due to their built-in revenue streams. Appraisers typically factor in future cash flows, increasing appraised value by 10–20%.

3. Marketability to Eco-Conscious Buyers

Sustainability is increasingly influencing purchasing decisions. Eco-friendly properties sell faster and appeal to companies aiming to meet Environmental, Social, and Governance (ESG) goals.

4. Dual Land Use Potential

In some cases, solar farms can coexist with agriculture, such as sheep grazing or low-height crop farming (agrivoltaics), allowing landowners to **maximize productivity**.

Key Statistics and Facts

- **30% Federal Investment Tax Credit (ITC)** remains in effect for many new solar projects through 2032.

- Over **250,000 acres of U.S. farmland** are under solar lease agreements as of 2023.

- The solar industry employs **over 250,000 Americans** and is growing annually.

- Average per-acre lease rates in high-demand areas (California, Texas, Florida) can exceed **$1,000 per acre per year**.

Financial Considerations and Tax Implications

Taxation of Lease Income

Solar lease income is typically taxed as ordinary income, not capital gains.

However, you can deduct:

- Attorney's fees

- Consulting fees

- Property maintenance costs

Speak with a tax advisor familiar with agricultural and renewable energy law.

Potential Property Tax Impacts

Solar installations may trigger reassessment under property tax laws. Some states, however, exempt solar improvements from property tax increases to encourage development.

Estate Planning Benefits

A long-term solar lease can enhance the financial security of future generations while preserving the land from high-impact industrial uses.

Risk Management and Protections

Decommissioning Provisions

Ensure your lease includes:

- Developer's obligation to remove all equipment

- Restoration of soil and vegetation

- Security deposits or bonds to guarantee decommissioning funds

Bankruptcy Protection

Include lease language that:

- Requires the developer to maintain financial assurances

- Allows you to regain full land control if a developer defaults

Insurance Requirements

Specify that the developer must carry:

- General liability insurance

- Environmental hazard coverage

- Property damage insurance

You should be named as an additional insured party.

Embracing the Solar Revolution: A Strategic Asset

Incorporating a solar farm can be part of a larger land management strategy, aligning sustainability goals with smart business practices.

Benefits to landowners include:

- Long-term passive income

- Preservation of open space

- Improved market positioning for green investors

Moreover, by contributing to clean energy, you leave a positive legacy in your community—one that combines stewardship with economic savvy.

Expanded Frequently Asked Questions (FAQs)

Will a solar farm decrease the value of neighboring properties?

Studies by Lawrence Berkeley National Laboratory and others suggest no consistent negative effect. In some cases, adjacent property values increased due to infrastructure improvements.

Can I continue to use my land after installing a solar farm?

Yes. Sheep grazing, beekeeping, pollinator gardens, and some forms of crop production are compatible with solar arrays, maximizing land use.

What happens when the lease ends?

Developers are obligated to remove panels, posts, wiring, and restore the land to a defined standard, as specified in the lease.

How long does it take to get a solar farm built after signing a lease?

Typically **18–36 months** depending on permitting complexity, grid connection studies, and construction schedules.

What are common challenges during development?

- Community opposition based on aesthetics

- Delays in obtaining interconnection approvals

- Environmental reviews revealing sensitive habitats

- Shifts in state renewable energy policies

What type of developer should I look for?

Prefer companies that:

- Have completed multiple similar projects

- Offer transparent lease terms

- Are financially stable and insured

Is a landowner responsible for environmental cleanup?

Typically, no. Developers must carry insurance and bond funds for cleanup under responsible solar development agreements.

Final Thoughts: Building a Renewable Future from the Ground Up

Landowners who take strategic action today position themselves at the leading edge of a massive global shift. Hosting a solar farm offers **stable, inflation-resistant income, increases property valuation, and contributes to the global clean energy movement.**

While the path involves diligence, negotiation, and community engagement, the rewards—financial, social, and environmental—are significant.

As the world shifts toward greener energy solutions, the sun isn't just shining on your land—it's offering you the opportunity to turn that sunlight into prosperity for generations to come.

Seize the moment. Invest in the future. Your land's best years may just be beginning.

FROGMAN MINDFULNESS

Jon Macaskill
US Navy SEAL Commander (Ret)
Keynote Speaking
One on One Coaching
Mindfulness Teaching
www.frogmanmindfulness.com
757-619-1211

Why Consistent Branding Is Key to Business Success

Your branding is what people first see when they interact with your business. This comes in the form of your identity, logo, color scheme, and messaging. It's the very first impression and is the real base for all customer interactions. If there's one thing that can help you succeed in business today, it's a consistent brand. It gives recognition, builds trust, and evokes loyalty from customers. This article explains the reasons behind consistent branding, its effects on your business, and how to maintain it.

Businesses and Brands

The state of California, specifically Los Angeles, is a beehive for businesses and brands booming with waves of diversity and competition. A dynamic economy coupled with an innovative attitude makes the city host to a smorgasbord of business industries: entertainment, technology, fashion, hospitality, and others.

Any business will find its way to success in a very competitive Los Angeles if only consistency and brand recognition are put into play. Partnering with a Los Angeles branding agency will offer the necessary skills and resources to establish a powerful, lasting presence. Such agencies deliver tailored solutions that would effectively communicate businesses' values to their customers, engage them, and be different from others. That shall drive growth and brand loyalty within the busy LA marketplace.

Building Brand Recognition

One of the major advantages of consistent branding deals with building brand recognition. When all brand elements across platforms and materials are consistent and coherent, it becomes easier for customers to recognize and remember your business. This is what makes the business stand out in a very crowded marketplace, keeping the business top-of-mind with consumers.

Visual Consistency

Visual consistency means using the same logo, colors, typography, and design elements across all marketing materials. These include your website, social media pages, business cards, advertising materials, and packaging. Consistency in visual identity will engage your web design in customers' minds and strengthen the memory of it.

Messaging Consistency

It ensures consistency for your brand's voice, tone, and key messages across all channels. From website copy to social media posts, email newsletters, and customer service interactions, consistency in messaging clearly communicates your brand's values and promises. This uniformity builds trust and reliability, facilitating customers to easily connect with your brand.

Messaging Consistency

It ensures consistency for your brand's voice, tone, and key messages across all channels. From website copy to social media posts, email newsletters, and customer service interactions, consistency in messaging clearly communicates your brand's values and promises. This uniformity builds trust and reliability, facilitating customers to easily connect with your brand.

Enhancing Marketing Efforts

Effective marketing is a requirement for business growth, and it's fueled by consistent branding. A cohesive brand identity will ensure all of your marketing materials work together to communicate your brand message and drive your business forward.

Integrated Campaigns

Such consistency is what leads to integrated marketing across different platforms. With homogeneous brand elements and messages, it gives customers a seamless experience whether they see the brand online, in-store, or through advertisement. These efforts are amplified through integration, ensuring a unified brand appearance.

Cost-Effective Marketing

It can also be cost-effective to have branding that is consistent. When you have a defined brand identity and set guidelines, things become easier for the production of marketing materials, because redesigns are reduced. This efficiency in time and resources can help you allocate your marketing budget more effectively.

Strong Brand Equity

Branding consistency is solidly linked with high brand equity. Brand equity is generally described as the value that a brand has in the marketplace. The more significant this equity, the more buyer preference for the brand over others in terms of recognition, trust, and use. This could then translate to gaining market share, increasing sales, and charging premium prices for the product or service.

Ways to Ensure Consistent Branding

In other words, consistent branding needs proper planning, implementation, and monitoring. Here are some ways to ensure your brand's consistency and effectiveness at every touchpoint.

Develop Brand Guidelines

One set of rules and standards specifies how your brand elements should be used, covering visual identity, messaging, tone of voice, and other brand features.

Regular Audits

Do regular audits on your branding materials. The website, social media profiles, sales collateral, or any other branded content should be checked against your brand guidelines for consistency. Regular audits help identify and address inconsistencies before they affect your brand image.

Training and Communication

Educate your team and stakeholders on the power of brand consistency, and train them in the process of working within your brand guidelines. This clearly communicates each person's role in maintaining brand consistency, how to locate resources or support when needed, and how to sustain consistency.

Use Technology

Leverage technology to make your branding more efficient. Brand management software will keep branding assets organized, allowing your team to know where to locate them and how to use them. Additionally, tools like social media management platforms and content scheduling software can ensure consistent branding across all digital channels.

Long-Term Benefits of Consistent Branding

Branding will prove to be a very good investment for your business in the long term. The benefits of branding extend beyond immediate recognition and trust, supporting long-term growth and success.

Higher Loyalty

This is bound to bring about customer loyalty since it creates a picture of dependability and reliability. The moment customers experience something great and consistent with your brand, then they will have a reason to be loyal and stick with your business. This may result in repeat purchases, positive word-of-mouth, and generally increased customer lifetime value.

Competitive Advantage

A strong and consistent brand will

Your clients will be more likely to choose you over your competition if your brand is known for professionalism, reliability, and a cohesive identity. This differentiation is most important in sectors where products or services are similar, so brand perception really comes into play in customer choice.

Brand Advocacy

This in turn makes them typically become brand ambassadors, freely propagating your business. There is an increase in advocacy through consistent branding since it shows the best parts of your brand. Since your customers understand what your brand is all about and continue to experience it over and over again, they likely refer your business to friends and family.

Business Growth

Ultimately, this means more business. A strong brand builds awareness, establishes trust, develops loyalty, and engenders advocacy—qualifications that empower it to drive sales, grow your customer base, and increase market share. This growth is sustainable because the foundation upon which it's based comprises strong, positive brand experiences that are repetitively consistent.

FAQs

How does consistent branding affect customer perception?

It reflects the image of professionalism and reliability, hence winning the trust of customers. This positive perception induces customers to choose your brand over others.

What are brand guidelines, and why are they important?

Brand guidelines refer to a set of rules or standards on how to use brand logos, colors, and messaging. This set of rules is important in ensuring there is consistency within all the materials that bear your brand identity.

How do I know my team is really using the brand guidelines?

Inform your team about the need for brand consistency and supply all the necessary training and tools. Also, regularly perform audits and attach clear lines of communication to help people actually follow brand guidelines.

Conclusion

Branding consistency has been one of the most essential ingredients for business success. It brings recognition, trust, and customer loyalty. Clearly, a consistent brand image will go a long way in the very competitive goods and services market by supporting the marketing efforts through their long-term growth.

Such activities as strategic planning, regular audits, and proper communication are highly relevant to developing and sustaining a consistent brand. This pays off definitely in the long run. In building a strong, consistent brand, be aware that these touchpoints occur in every level of interaction with your audience to reinforce brand identity and create a long-term relationship.

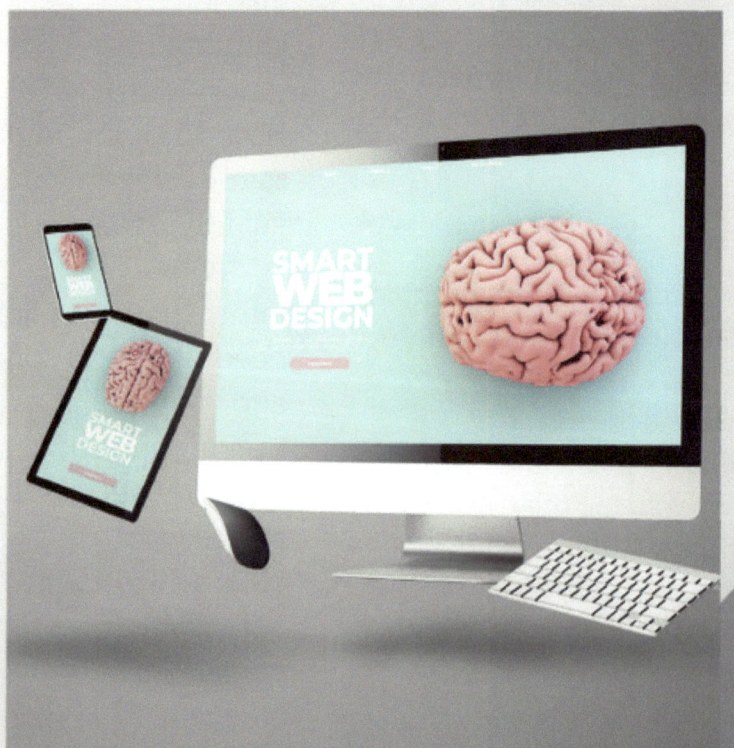

www.ingramcontent.com/pod-product-compliance
Lightning Source LLC
Chambersburg PA
CBHW041703200326
41518CB00002B/173